MW01622782

LEWITT X 2

SOL LEWITT: STRUCTURE AND LINE

SELECTIONS FROM THE LEWITT COLLECTION

Organized by Dean Swanson   *Essays by Dean Swanson and Martin Friedman*

MADISON MUSEUM OF CONTEMPORARY ART

MADISON MUSEUM OF CONTEMPORARY ART

Generous funding for *LeWitt x 2* has been provided by the Steinhauer Charitable Trust; J.H. Findorff & Son Inc.; Peggy Hedberg and John Niederhuber; John Neis and Chele Isaac; the Dane County Cultural Affairs Commission with additional funds from the Endres Mfg. Company Foundation and the Overture Foundation; the Terry Family Foundation; the Art League of the Madison Museum of Contemporary Art; and a grant from the Wisconsin Arts Board with funds from the State of Wisconsin.

Published for the exhibtion *LeWitt x 2*
organized by the Madison Museum of Contemporary Art.

Madison Museum of Contemporary Art, Madison, Wisconsin
November 5, 2006–January 14, 2007

Miami Art Museum, Miami, Florida
February 9–June 3, 2007

Weatherspoon Art Museum, The University of North Carolina at Greensboro
September 9, 2007–January 18, 2008

Austin Museum of Art, Austin, Texas
May 24–August 17, 2008

Madison Museum of Contemporary Art
227 State Street
Madison, WI 53703
www.mmoca.org

A Braille version of this catalogue is available upon request.
Please contact the Madison Museum of Contemporary Art Education Department.

ISBN 0-913883-33-6

Library of Congress Control Number
2006930195

Distributed by
D.A.P./Distributed Art Publishers
155 6th Avenue, 2nd Floor
New York, NY 10013
T: 212-627-1999
F: 212-627-9484
www.artbook.com

Designer
Lorraine Ferguson

Manuscript Editor
Joseph N Newland, Q.E.D.

Project Coordinator
Jane Simon

Editors
Susanna Singer
Janet Passehl

Printed in China by Oceanic Graphic Press, in an edition of 2000

All works illustrated are in The LeWitt Collection unless otherwise noted.
In stated dimensions, height precedes width precedes depth.

Front cover
Sol LeWitt (American, b. 1928)
HORIZONTAL LINES 2005
Gouache on paper
60 x 58 ½ inches

Back cover
Franz West (Austrian, b. 1947)
Untitled (Sphairos) 1988
Painted paper-mâché
15 x 14 x 20 inches

CONTENTS

DIRECTOR'S FOREWORD

Stephen Fleischman

Director
Madison Museum of Contemporary Art

Beginning in the 1960s Sol LeWitt began to collect the work of fellow artists. As the influence of his own work took on international proportions so did the collection he continued to build. His acquisitions often provided important encouragement and support to emerging artists at pivotal moments in their careers. Since the 1980s LeWitt has been joined in the collection's assembly by his wife, Carol Androccio LeWitt.

LeWitt x 2 is a two-part exhibition. It presents works by Sol LeWitt, ranging from early structures to a sampling of his most recent gouaches. These works demonstrate his strong contributions to conceptual and minimalist art as well as more recent explorations of brightly hued curvilinear forms.

The second component of *LeWitt x 2* emphasizes the breadth and strength of the collection of works by other artists assembled by the LeWitts. It reflects the close relationships that they have established with artists and examines the wide range of artistic sensibilities, media, and ideas represented in their collection.

My deepest thanks go to Sol and Carol LeWitt. Their talent, collecting acumen, and generosity of spirit in lending their collection have ensured the success of this project. Guest curator Dean Swanson has overseen every aspect of the exhibition and this publication with extraordinary skill. I also extend my appreciation to guest author Martin Friedman for his essay based on his long friendship with Sol LeWitt.

Generous funding for *LeWitt x 2* has been provided by the Steinhauer Charitable Trust; J.H. Findorff & Son Inc.; Peggy Hedberg and John Niederhuber; John Neis and Chele Isaac; the Dane County Cultural Affairs Commission with additional funds from the Endres Mfg. Company Foundation and the Overture Foundation; the Terry Family Foundation; the Art League of the Madison Museum of Contemporary Art; and a grant from the Wisconsin Arts Board with funds from the State of Wisconsin.

It has been gratifying to collaborate with several venues that are participating in the tour of *LeWitt x 2*. Special thanks are due to Terence Riley, Director, and Peter Boswell, Assistant Director for Programs/Senior Curator, at the Miami Art Museum as well as Nancy Doll, Director at the Weatherspoon Art Museum, at the University of North Carolina at Greensboro; and Dana Friis-Hansen, the Dr. and Mrs. Ernest C. Butler Executive Director, and Eva Buttacavoli, Director of Exhibitions and Education, at the Austin Museum of Art. This publication was greatly enhanced by the talents of Lorraine Ferguson, graphic designer; Joseph N. Newland, manuscript editor; and the photography of John Groo.

I wish to thank the Madison Museum of Contemporary Art's Board of Trustees for its continuing support and enthusiasm. It is also my pleasure to thank the entire museum staff for their dedicated work in bringing this project to fruition.

LeWitt x 2 continues a MMoCA tradition of organizing significant exhibitions for travel. The museum is honored to have this exhibition on view in its commodious, new galleries.

ACKNOWLEDGMENTS

Dean Swanson

My enthusiasm for Sol LeWitt's art began when I first saw the work around 1970, and my admiration has only grown over the years as fresh ideas and new expressions have appeared. It has been a great pleasure talking to Sol and his wife, Carol Androccio LeWitt, as this exhibition has developed. Their kindness, patience, and commitment to sharing their extraordinary collection has given the project a unique and personal character.

From the beginning, this has been planned as a two-part presentation—a group of works by Sol LeWitt shown in tandem with selections from the extraordinary LeWitt Collection. I am grateful to the LeWitts for generously lending all of the works in both portions of the exhibition.

Susanna Singer plays an important role in all projects concerning Sol LeWitt's work. As his long-standing representative, she and her assistant James Martin have once again served an important editorial review function for this publication.

Over the past three years, I have worked with Janet Passehl, curator and registrar of The LeWitt Collection. This exhibition is significantly better because of Janet's familiarity with the works and her excellent judgement. I am also grateful to her assistant, John Lavertu, for his dedication to this project.

Martin Friedman has contributed an essay to this publication which perfectly captures the respect and affection of Sol LeWitt's artist friends. In preparing this essay, he talked with Carl Andre, Chuck Close, Barry Le Va, Robert Mangold, Sylvia Plimack Mangold, Dorothea Rockburne, and Pat Steir. He also spoke with former Curator of Contemporary Art at the Wadsworth Atheneum Museum of Art, Andrea Miller-Keller, who used works from The LeWitt Collection in numerous exhibitions, and Jo Watanabe, who has executed many of LeWitt's wall drawings. He would also like to acknowledge the help of Susan Packard in the preparation of his manuscript; Gene Gaddis, the archivist at the Wadsworth Atheneum Museum of Art; and, at the Walker Art Center, the librarian Rosemary Furtak, the archivist Jill Vetter, and the visual resources librarian Stephanie Kays.

It has been a great pleasure working with the staff of the Madison Museum of Contemporary Art. Stephen Fleischman, the Museum's Director, has enthusiastically encouraged and facilitated this project. Among his administrative talents is the assembly of an excellent staff. I am especially grateful to Jane Simon, Curator of Exhibitions, who has been involved in many aspects of the organization of the exhibition and coordinated the publication. Registrar Marilyn Sohi efficiently oversaw the details of shipping and handling the works of art, and Curatorial Assistant Emily Schreiner expeditiously helped with preparation of catalogue copy.

CUBE 1997
Gouache on paper
60 ½ × 60 ½ inches

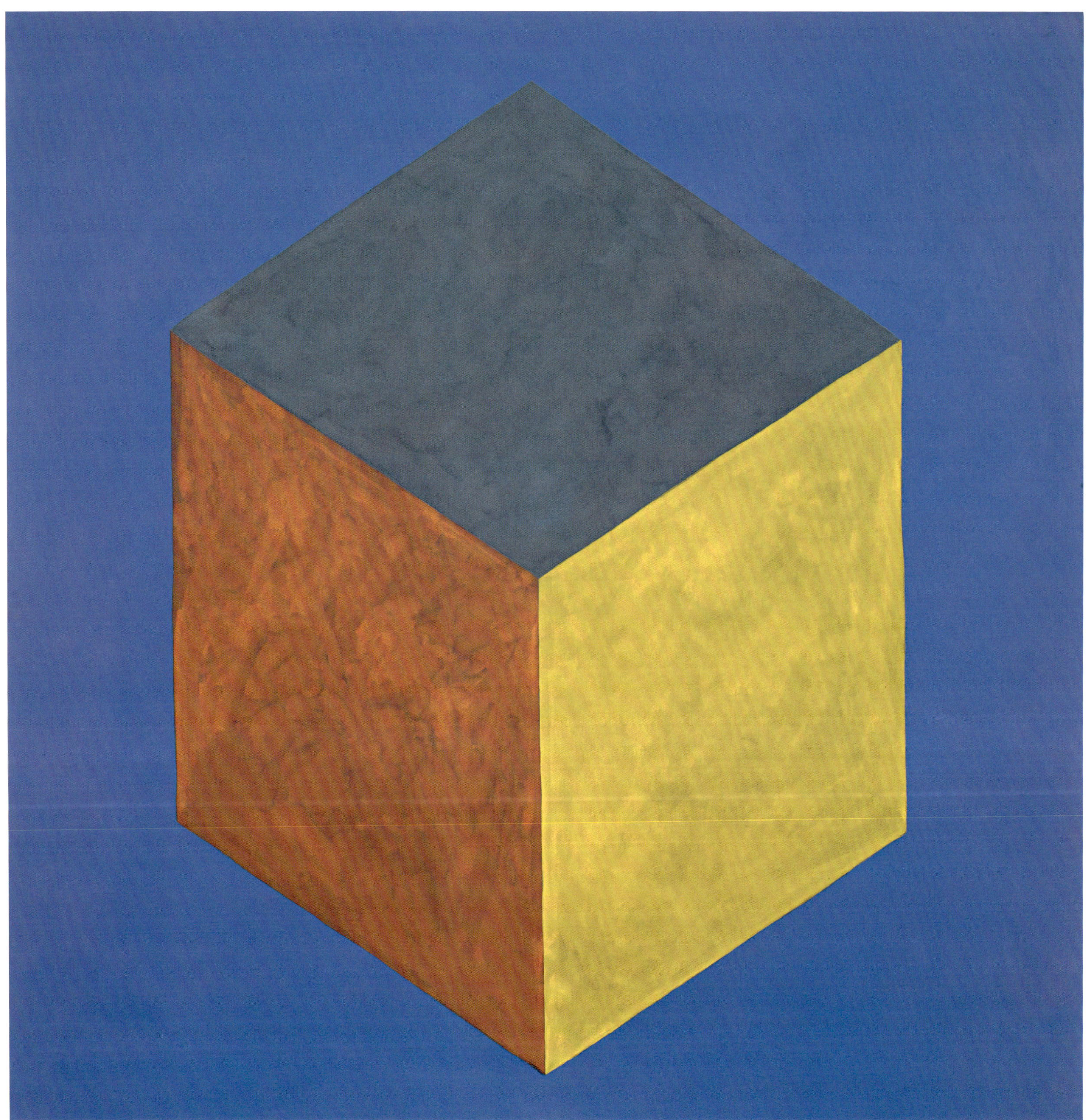

STRUCTURE AND LINE

Dean Swanson

Ideas cannot be owned.
They belong to whomever understands them.
Sol LeWitt [1]

These words express a selflessness and generosity that are at the core of Sol LeWitt's art. In all its forms, it is accessible. It belongs to us. This exhibition focuses on two essential aspects of LeWitt's art, works on paper and "structures," the term he uses for his three-dimensional pieces. The richness and variety of his production is represented here in artworks made over four decades.

LeWitt was born in Hartford, Connecticut, in 1928. At age six, following the death of his father, a physician, he moved with his mother to nearby New Britain. Upon graduation from New Britain High School, he entered Syracuse University as an art major, and he graduated in 1949. A Tiffany grant funded a semester at the University of Illinois, where LeWitt was a teaching assistant, and in 1950 he traveled in Europe. The following year he was drafted and served in Japan and Korea, during the Korean War. After leaving the Army, LeWitt moved to New York City.

By the mid-1950s, New York had become the undisputed center of the contemporary art world and occupied a position similar to that of Paris in the early twentieth century. The work of the Abstract Expressionist painters (Jackson Pollock, Willem de Kooning, Robert Motherwell, Barnett Newman, Mark Rothko, and others) was an established success, and many followers continued to work in the gestural style of the "action painting" of the New York School.

LeWitt attended classes and had several jobs in the field of graphic design, including a stint in the newly opened office of the architect I.M. Pei. Working in an architectural firm, he observed that the development of a design concept can be completely separate from the execution of that idea by others, a model that was to have an effect on his future method. LeWitt himself was making heavily brushed abstract paintings, yet he was dissatisfied with his work. After quitting his job at the Pei office, he concentrated for a time on drawing, and in 1958 made a group of ink sketches based on familiar Old Master paintings by Piero della Francesca, Diego Velasquez, Jean-Auguste-Dominique Ingres, and others. Throughout the years, he has often made drawings as a way of clarifying his ideas and developing works in other media.

In 1960 LeWitt began working at the Museum of Modern Art, at the book sales desk, and later as a night receptionist. Among his coworkers were other young artists such as Dan Flavin, Robert Ryman, and Robert Mangold, who worked as guards, and the writer Lucy Lippard, who was to become an influential critic later in the decade. LeWitt was now living on Hester Street in Lower Manhattan, and his neighbors included Lippard and Ryman as well as artists Eva Hesse and Tom Doyle. When Lucy Lippard looked back at this period in her 1973 book *Six Years: The Dematerialization of the Art Object,* she wrote that Sol LeWitt had been her "major intellectual influence at the time."[2]

Discussions among LeWitt and his circle of friends centered on a shared desire to find a way to make art that would be free of emotionalism and subjectivity. For these young artists, Abstract Expressionism had been played out. Intriguing alternatives were suggested in a 1960 exhibition organized by Dorothy C. Miller at the Museum of Modern Art, *16 Americans*, which included work by, among others, Jasper Johns, Robert Rauschenberg, Ellsworth Kelly, and Frank Stella. Another significant event was the publication in 1962 of Camilla Gray's *The Great Experiment: Russian Art 1863–1922*, which treated the work of Constructivist and Suprematist artists such as El Lissitzky, Aleksandr Rodchenko, and Vladimir Tatlin.[3] LeWitt has identified Russian Constructivism as an important influence on the development of his early work.

In his paintings of the early 1960s LeWitt moved from brushed abstractions to compositions in which sequences of small figures appear in series across the surface. In some of these, holes are cut out of the painting to reveal the figures, in what seems to be an attempt to resolve the nagging problem of the relationship between the object and the wall it hangs on. In 1963 LeWitt made painted reliefs, some wall-mounted, others suspended from the ceiling, in which geometric forms protrude into the room. That same year he made several freestanding, boxlike constructions of plywood over a supporting lumber framework. Then, in 1964, he built an "open" structure which eliminated the outer plywood membrane and revealed the frame beneath.

LeWitt's first solo exhibition took place in 1965 at Dan Graham's John Daniels Gallery in New York. He showed floor structures made of wooden slabs that met at right and oblique angles. These were early manifestations of the open cube forms that would frequently appear in his work. But it was the boxes with their exposed skeletal supports that LeWitt developed next. He decided to arrange them (the supports) in equal modules, making the lumber members and their crosspieces form a series of squares. As the squares project in three dimensions, the squares become cubes.

The wall-mounted structure in this exhibition is an early example of the open cube, which has been a consistent, often repeated form in LeWitt's work since the mid-1960s. It is painted white to minimize what he considered the distracting expressive texture of the wood and to visually integrate the structure with the white wall behind it. Subsequent open cube structures have also been executed in aluminum spray-painted white, and since the 1970s have been fabricated by others. He settled on a ratio of 1 to 8.5 for the width of the lumber to the space between members, and it has remained constant since that time.

Sol LeWitt is often identified as a key figure in Minimalist sculpture, along with Carl Andre, Dan Flavin, Donald Judd, and Robert Morris. However, only a few of LeWitt's early structures truly qualify as minimal works. A significant new direction in LeWitt's art occurred in 1966 with an installation of open and closed cubes arranged in a grid on the floor. The result, *Serial Project No.1 (ABCD),* is based on a set of permutations, or step-by-step modifications, of the basic cube form, laid out in series according to a pre-determined system.

SERIAL PROJECT #1 (ABCD) 1966–68
Baked enamel on steel
9 ½ x 70 x 70 inches
Collection Westfalisches Landesmueum, Münster, Germany

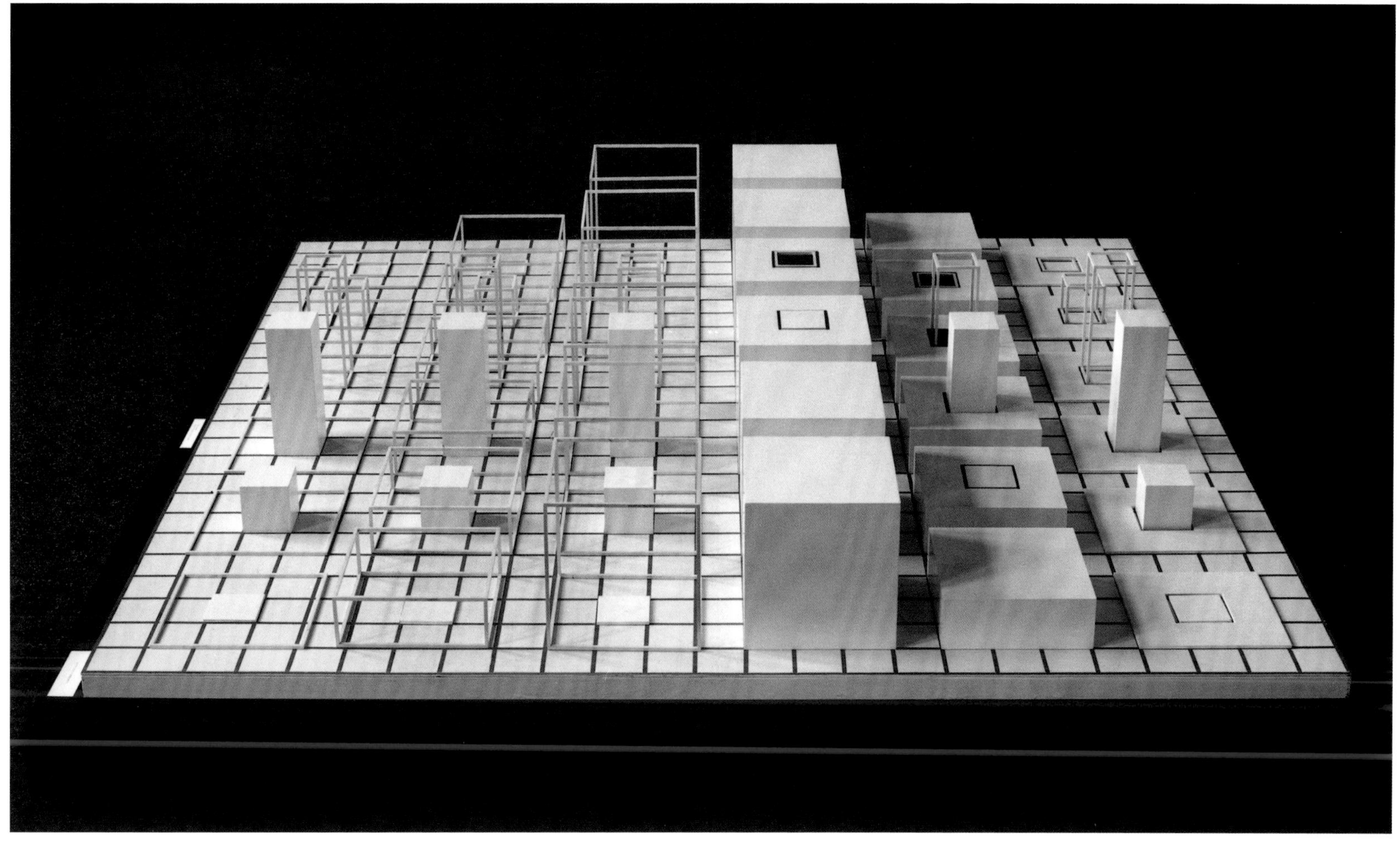

DRAWING SERIES I-1/3241/A AND B 1968
Ink on paper
10 ¼ x 20 ¾ inches

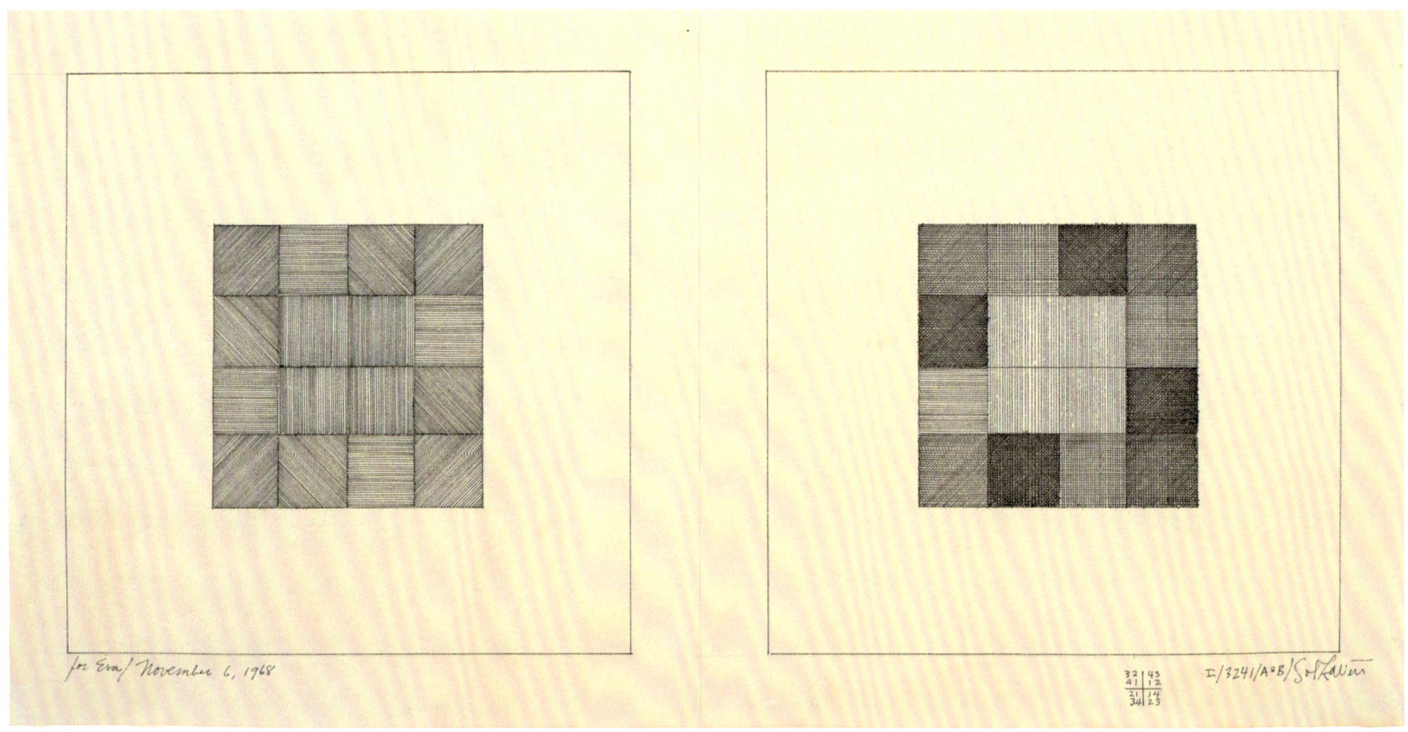

In 1967 LeWitt wrote "Paragraphs On Conceptual Art," which was published in *Artforum* magazine. A companion document, "Sentences On Conceptual Art," appeared in 1969 in *Art-Language*.[4] An essential theme of these observations is that the art-making process need not involve arbitrary or capricious decisions if a rational plan has been determined in advance.

LeWitt was one of several artists invited to participate in a 1968 project known as "the Xerox Book" (the others were Carl Andre, Robert Barry, Douglas Huebler, Joseph Kosuth, Robert Morris, and Lawrence Weiner);[5] it was planned as a publication that could be cheaply produced and distributed. Each artist was to fill twenty-five pages with work that made use of the eponymous photocopying process. LeWitt made a series of ink drawings employing a spare vocabulary of straight, ruled lines. The lines are horizontal, vertical, and diagonal in two directions, and they form squares, which he rotated according to a system of twenty-four permutations of 1/2/3/4. The twenty-fifth page summarized the twenty-four combinations of images. Like the simple cubes in LeWitt's structures, squares are familiar, instantly comprehensible visual elements that allow us to go directly to an understanding of the system that has determined them.

LeWitt's presence in the Xerox Book project, and his customary identification with conceptualist artists, requires clarification. Lucy Lippard pointed out that LeWitt made a distinction at the time between Conceptualism "with a capital C," which referred to art that is ephemeral, dematerialized, cheaply produced,

ALL TWO-PART COMBINATIONS OF LINES IN FOUR DIRECTIONS AND FOUR COLORS 1970
Marker and pencil on paper
11 ¾ x 19 ½ inches

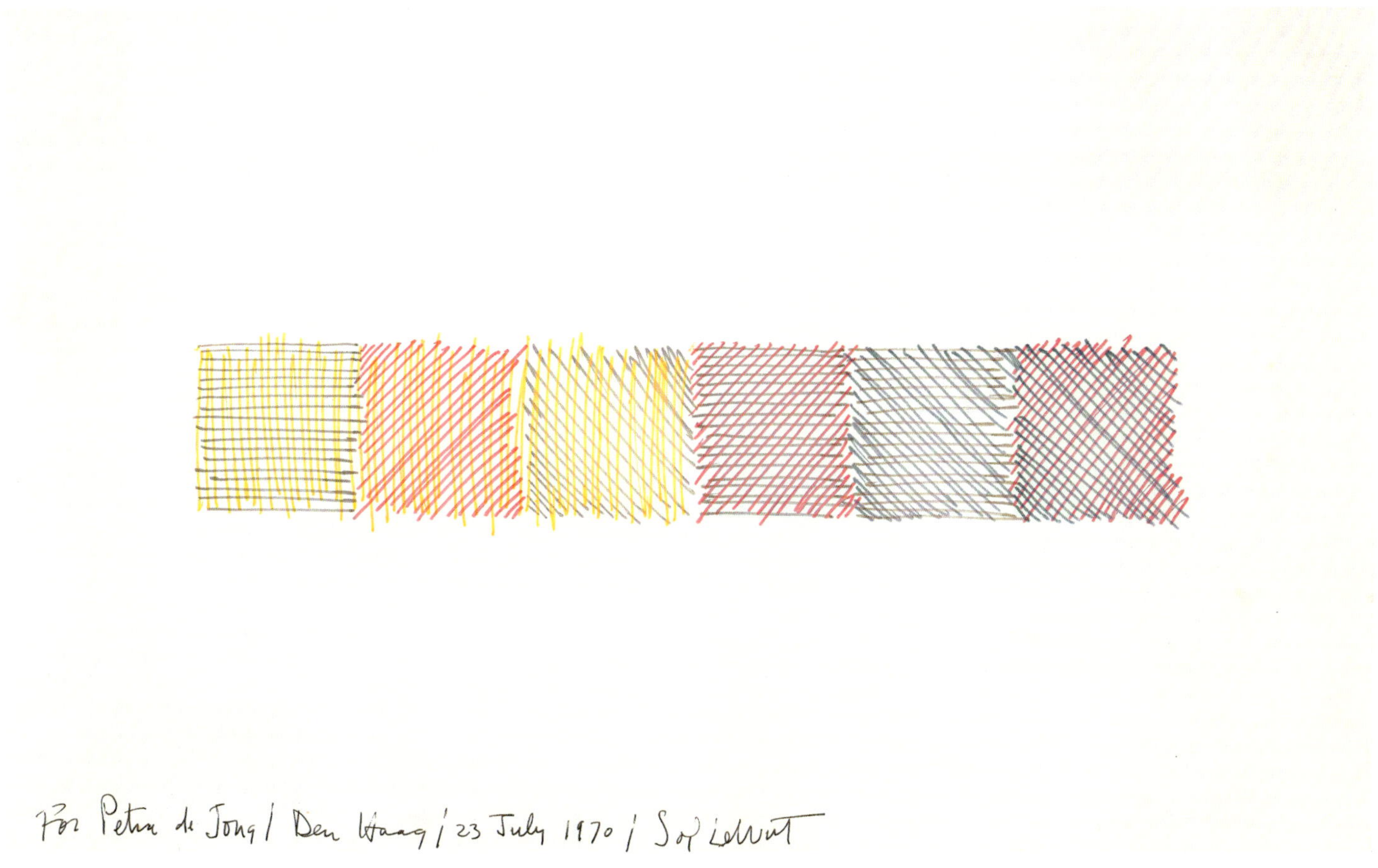

and information oriented, and conceptualism "with a small c," as in his work, "in which the material forms were often conventional, although generated by a paramount idea."[6]

What happened next was a dramatic leap forward that significantly shaped LeWitt's artistic future. In October 1968, he drew, at a larger scale and in pencil, on a wall at the Paula Cooper Gallery, part of the drawing series he had made for the Xerox Book. The implications of eliminating the traditional support for a drawn image (a sheet of paper, under glass in a frame that hangs on the wall) suggests not only a new relationship between art and the viewer, but a new relationship between art and architecture.

LeWitt executed the first wall drawings himself. Then, true to the views expressed in the "Paragraphs" and the "Sentences," he began to write instructions for the drawings, which could theoretically be carried out by anyone, on any wall. The idea is the work of art. Ever since he has entrusted the execution of the wall drawings to others. Over time, the wall drawings have become more site specific.

LeWitt's drawings on paper frequently relate to the wall drawings. In the 1970s, circles and arcs joined lines in his expanding visual vocabulary. Typical instructions for a wall drawing would include elements such as those identified in the title of the 1973 drawing *All Combinations of Arcs from Corners and Sides, Straight Lines, Not-Straight Lines, and Broken Lines.*

ALL COMBINATIONS OF ARCS FROM CORNERS AND SIDES, STRAIGHT LINES, NOT-STRAIGHT LINES, AND BROKEN LINES 1973
Ink and pencil on paper
17 ¼ x 17 ¼ inches

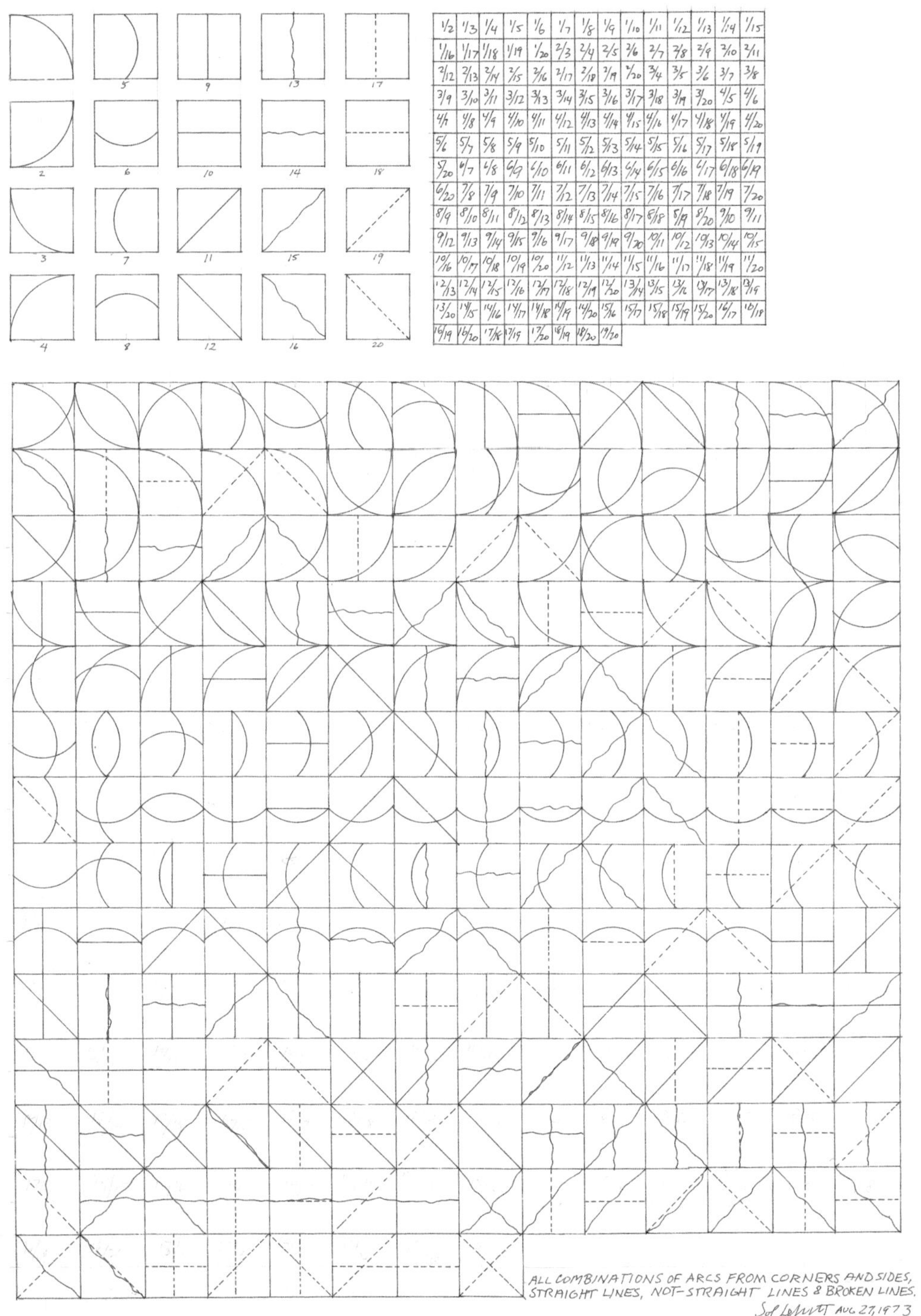

WALL DRAWING #260 ON BLACK WALLS, ALL TWO-PART COMBINATIONS OF WHITE ARCS FROM CORNERS AND SIDES, AND WHITE STRAIGHT, NOT STRAIGHT, AND BROKEN LINES 1975

White crayon, black pencil grid, black wall

First drawn by Sol LeWitt

First installation San Francisco Museum of Modern Art, San Francisco, California

Collection The Museum of Modern Art, New York, New York

Photographed at the Addison Gallery of American Art, Phillips Academy, Andover, Massachusetts

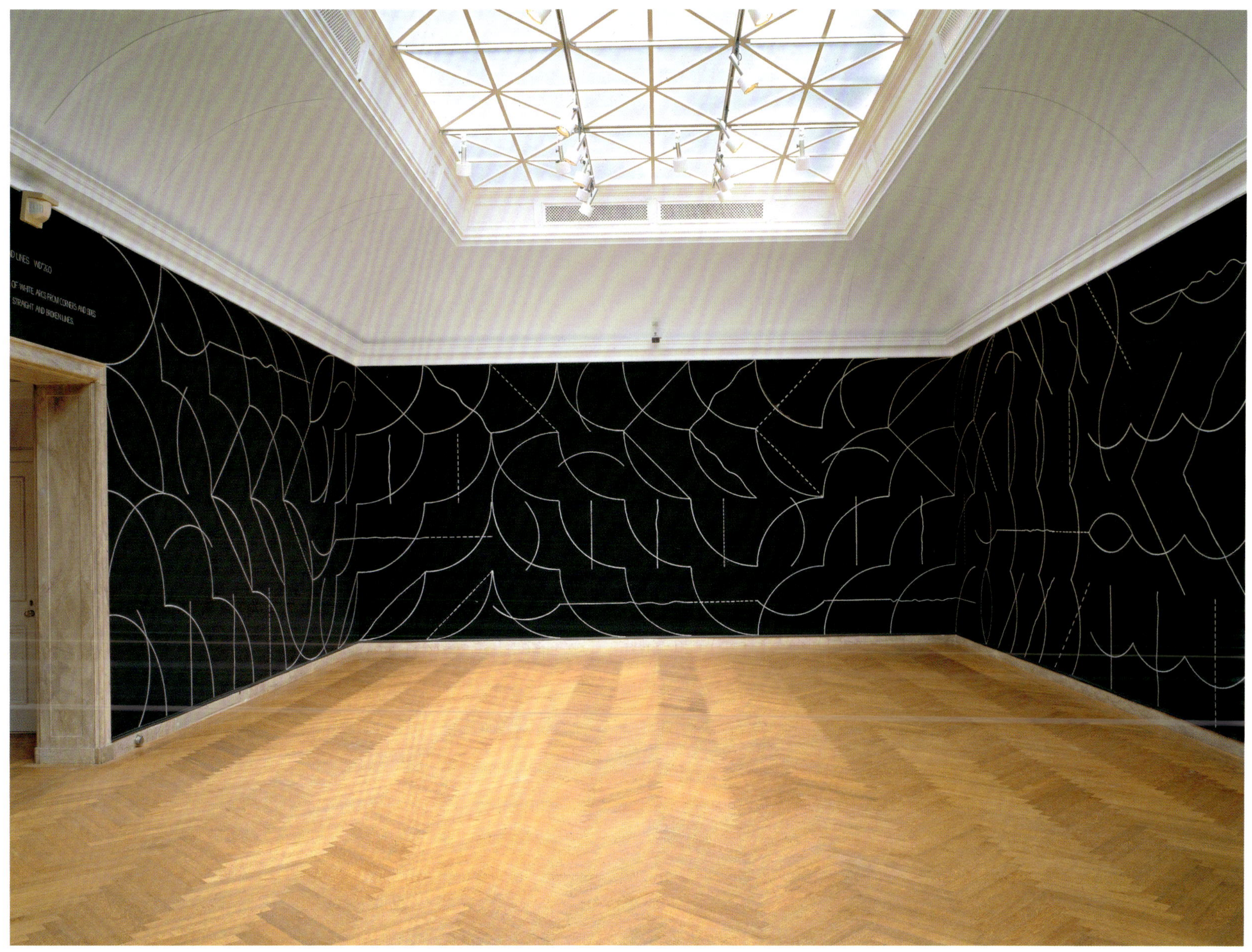

DRAWING FOR OPEN CUBE STRUCTURE 1971
Ink and pencil on paper
14 ½ x 12 inches

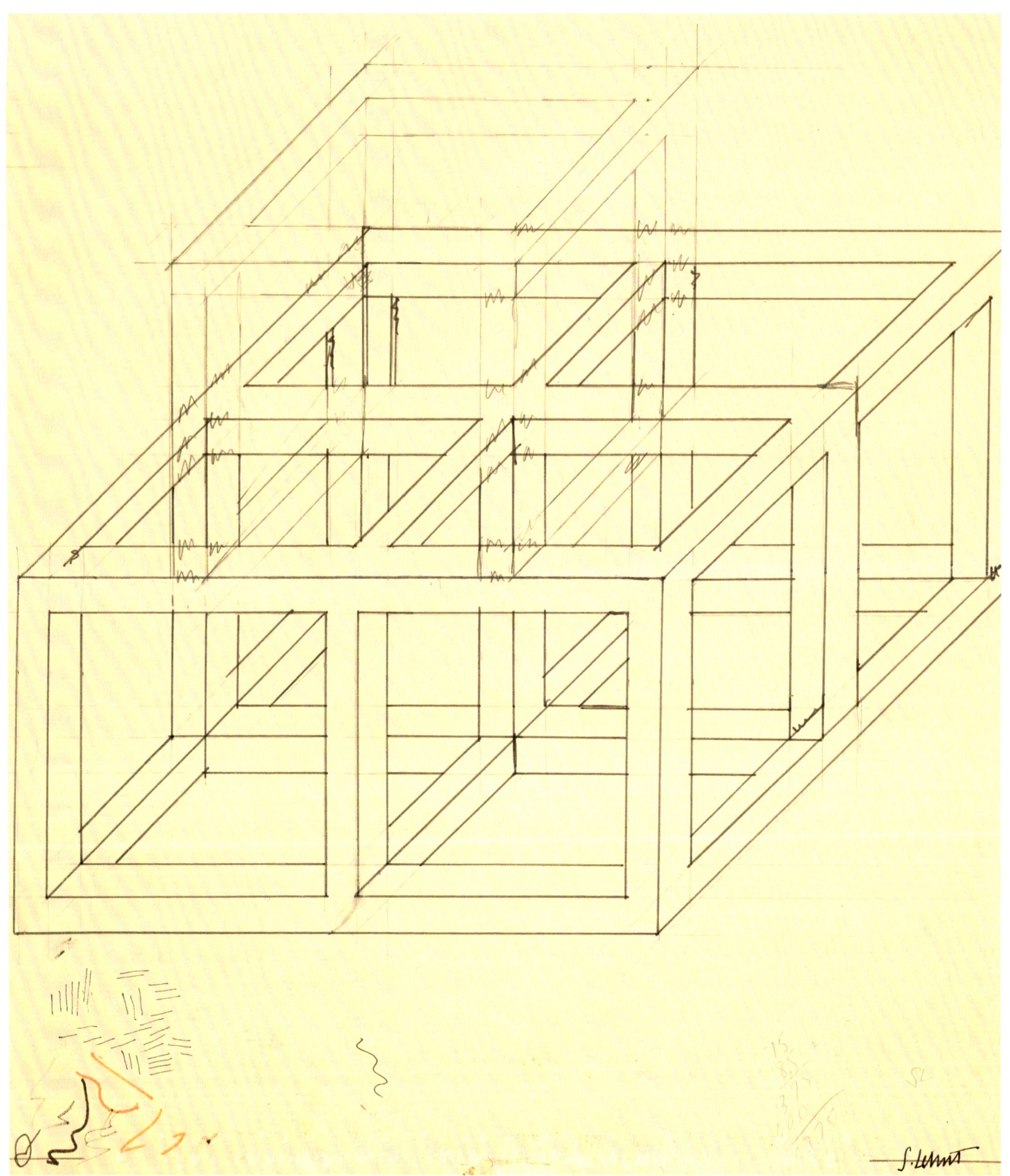

OPEN GEOMETRIC STRUCTURE 2-2 1-1 1991
Painted wood
20 × 29 ½ × 20 inches

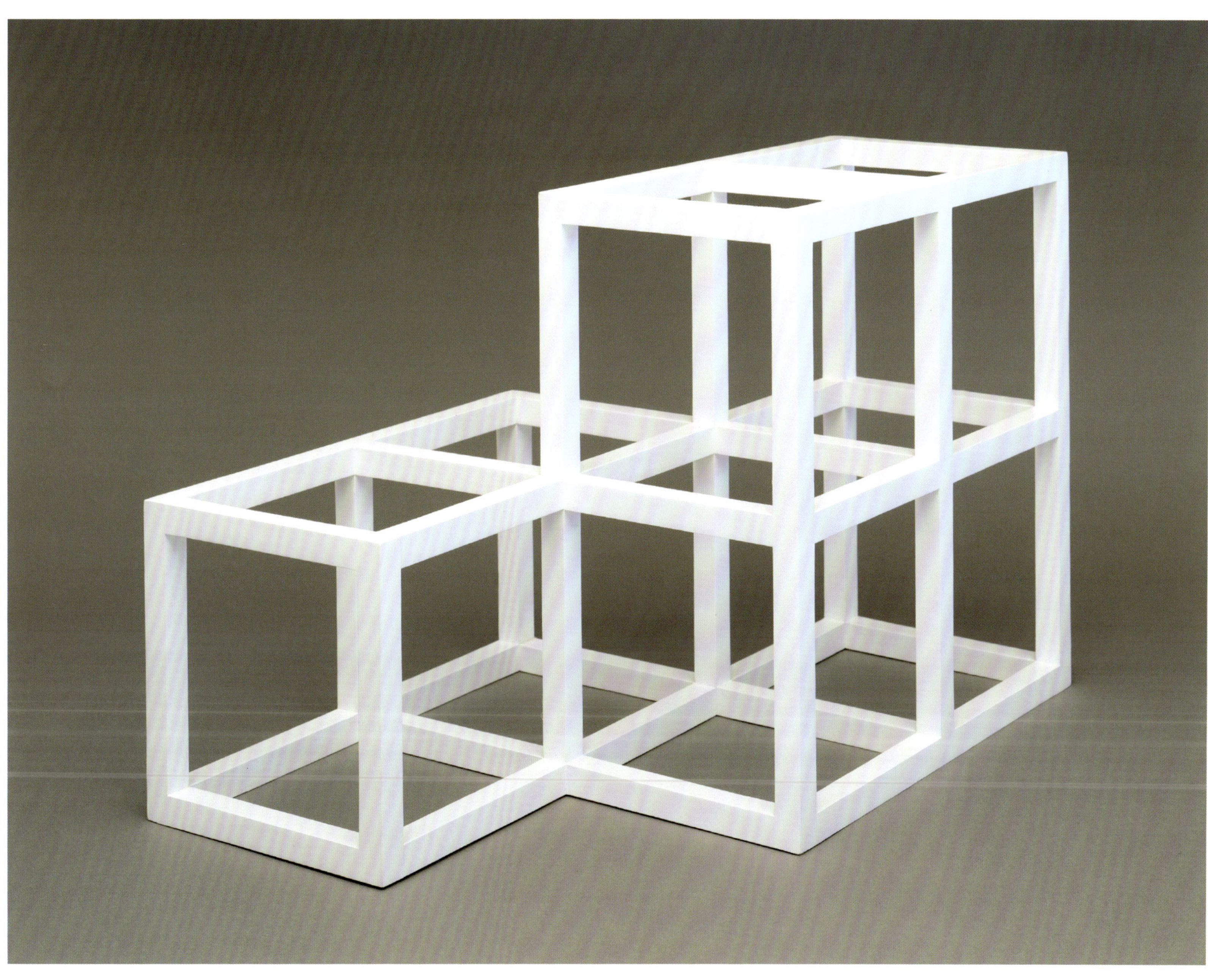

In *Drawing for Open Cube Structure* (1971) LeWitt has planned out a simple arrangement of a few identical open cubes, the form which has reappeared in many versions since its inception in the 1960s. Whether clustered in groups of a few units or multiplied many times in intricate, lacelike configurations, as in later pieces, the open cube has become a staple of the LeWitt oeuvre. Open cube structures have been fashioned in painted wood, and in steel and aluminum with a baked-on finish, always white (after a few in black). A variation on the form is the incomplete open cube, which has a vertex, or vertices, removed.

ISOMETRIC DRAWING, from a set of 40 1981
Ink on paper
19 × 19 inches

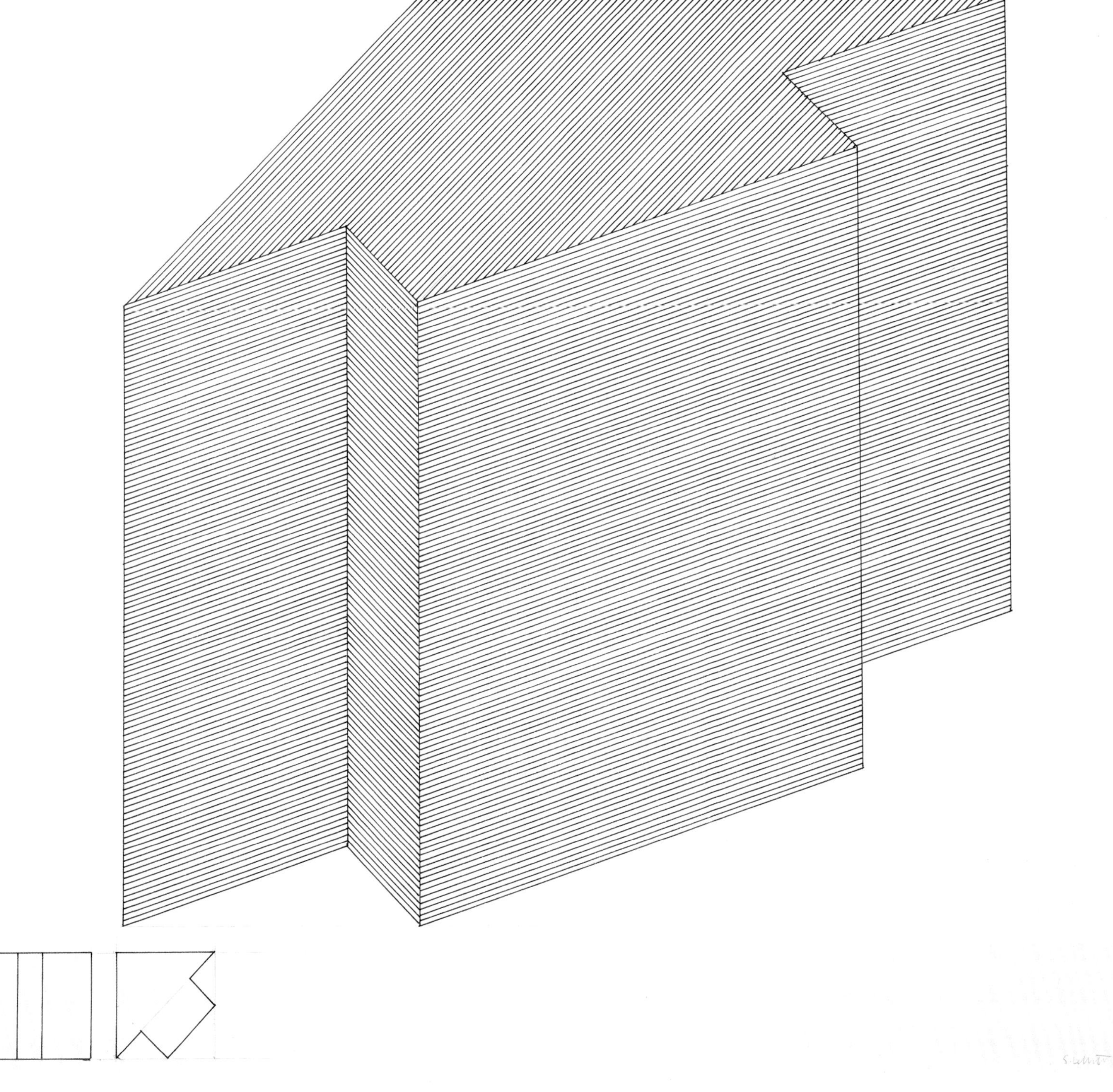

HORIZONTAL AND VERTICAL BANDS OF COLOR 1990
Gouache, pencil on paper
16 ½ × 29 ½ inches

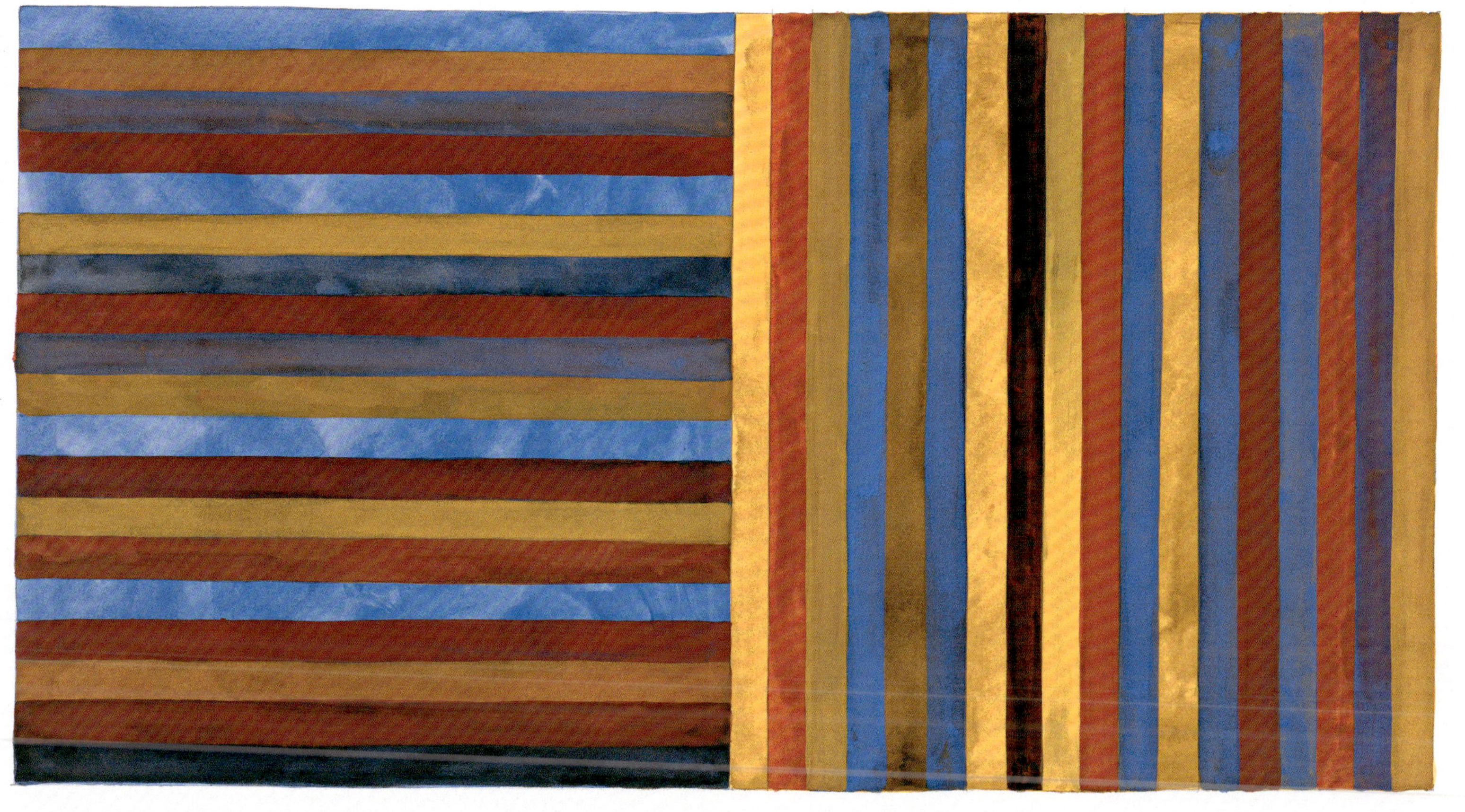

HORIZONTAL PROGRESSION #3 1991
Sprayed enamel on aluminum
18 ¼ × 81 ¼ × 18 ¼ inches

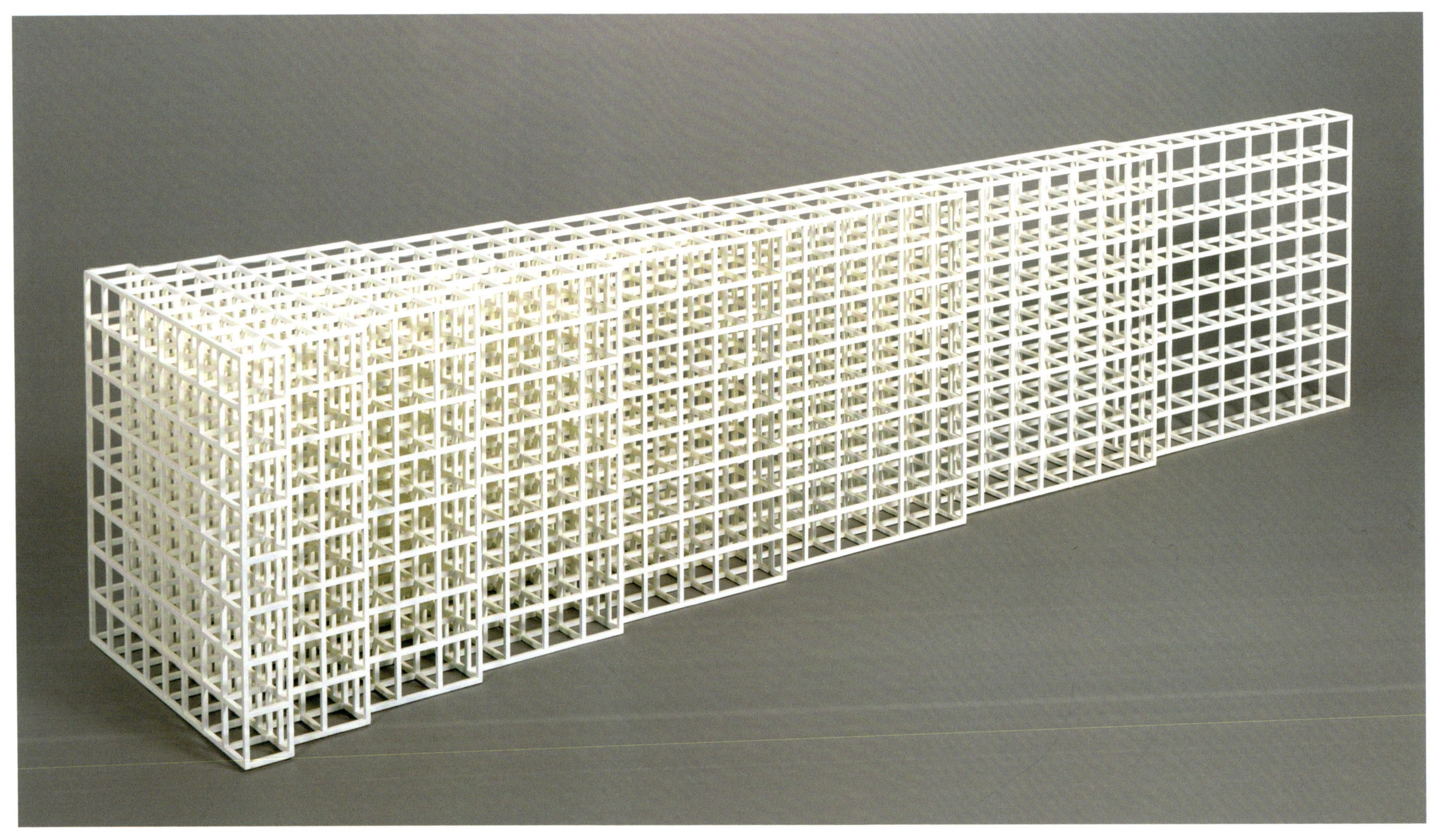

FORM DERIVED FROM A CUBIC RECTANGLE 1991
Gouache on paper
22 ¼ × 29 ¾ inches

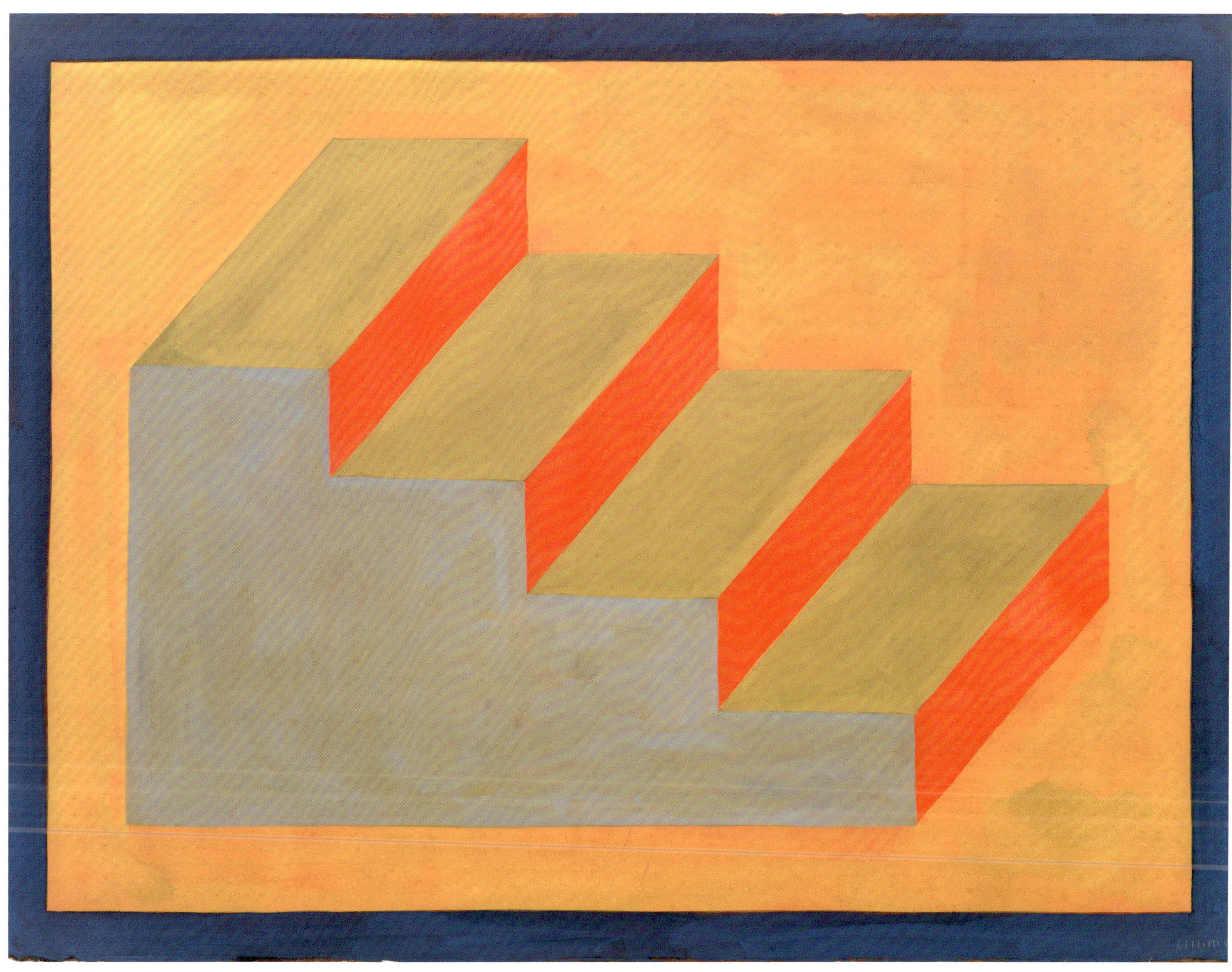

In the early 1980s LeWitt introduced more geometric forms—triangles, parallelograms, and so forth—in works on paper and on the wall. A major innovation of the same period is the use of brilliant color in the wall drawings. Made with an ink wash technique (which is executed by LeWitt's own assistants), these luminous walls have a rich depth that recalls Renaissance Italian frescoes. They have their counterpart in contemporaneous drawings on paper rendered in gouache, another medium that was then new to LeWitt's work. The geometric figures became isometric projections, as in *Pyramids,* in *Cubes,* and in a series called *Forms Derived from Cubic Rectangles* that followed.

IRREGULAR FORM 1998
Gouache on paper
22 ½ × 30 inches

In the mid-1980s, LeWitt began to make structures with a new material. Concrete block, readily available and comparatively inexpensive, could be used out-of-doors and assembled by workers with modest skills. The artist liked the idea of a material that had no historical association with art and could be worked in a monumental scale. The first concrete block structures were simple, cubical forms, but LeWitt soon expanded the repertoire to include towers, walls, pyramids, and clusters that suggest entire cities. In the summer of 2005, two large concrete block structures were erected in Madison Square Park in Lower Manhattan.

Exuberant color continued to appear in the gouaches throughout the 1990s, as LeWitt explored images that moved away from geometry in series such as the *Irregular Forms* and the colorful *Brushstrokes*. By the end of the decade, the wall drawings were being executed in brilliant acrylic paints.
In 1999, he experimented with applying the acrylic paints to a group of eccentrically shaped fiberglass structures he called *Non-Geometric Forms*. These evolved into the *Splotches*, of which there is a black-and-white example in this exhibition.

IRREGULAR GRID 1999
Gouache on paper
60 ½ x 61 ½ inches

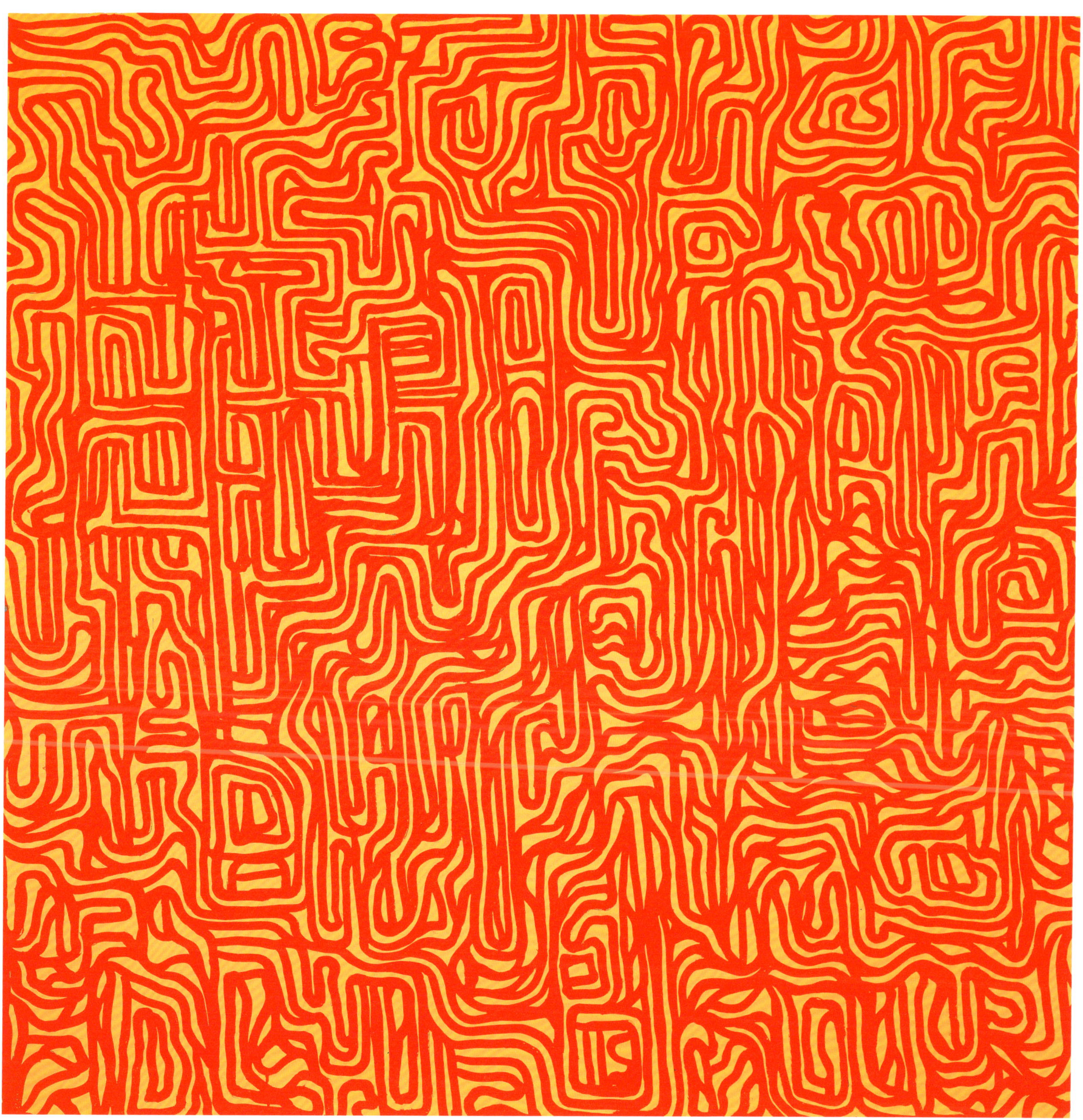

BRUSHSTROKES 2000
Gouache on paper
22 ½ × 29 ½ inches

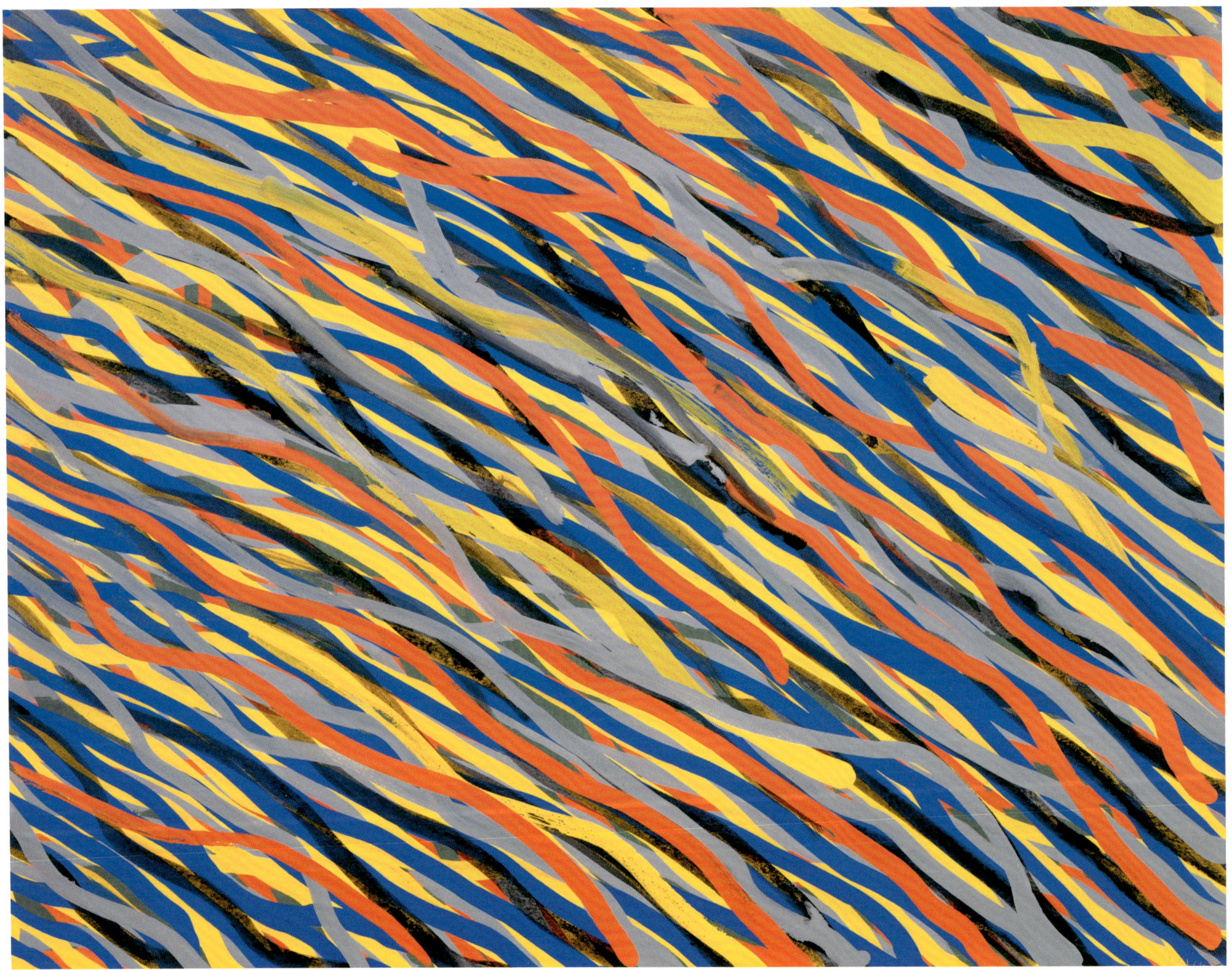

HORIZONTAL LINES 1997–2005
Gouache on paper
22 ½ × 30 inches

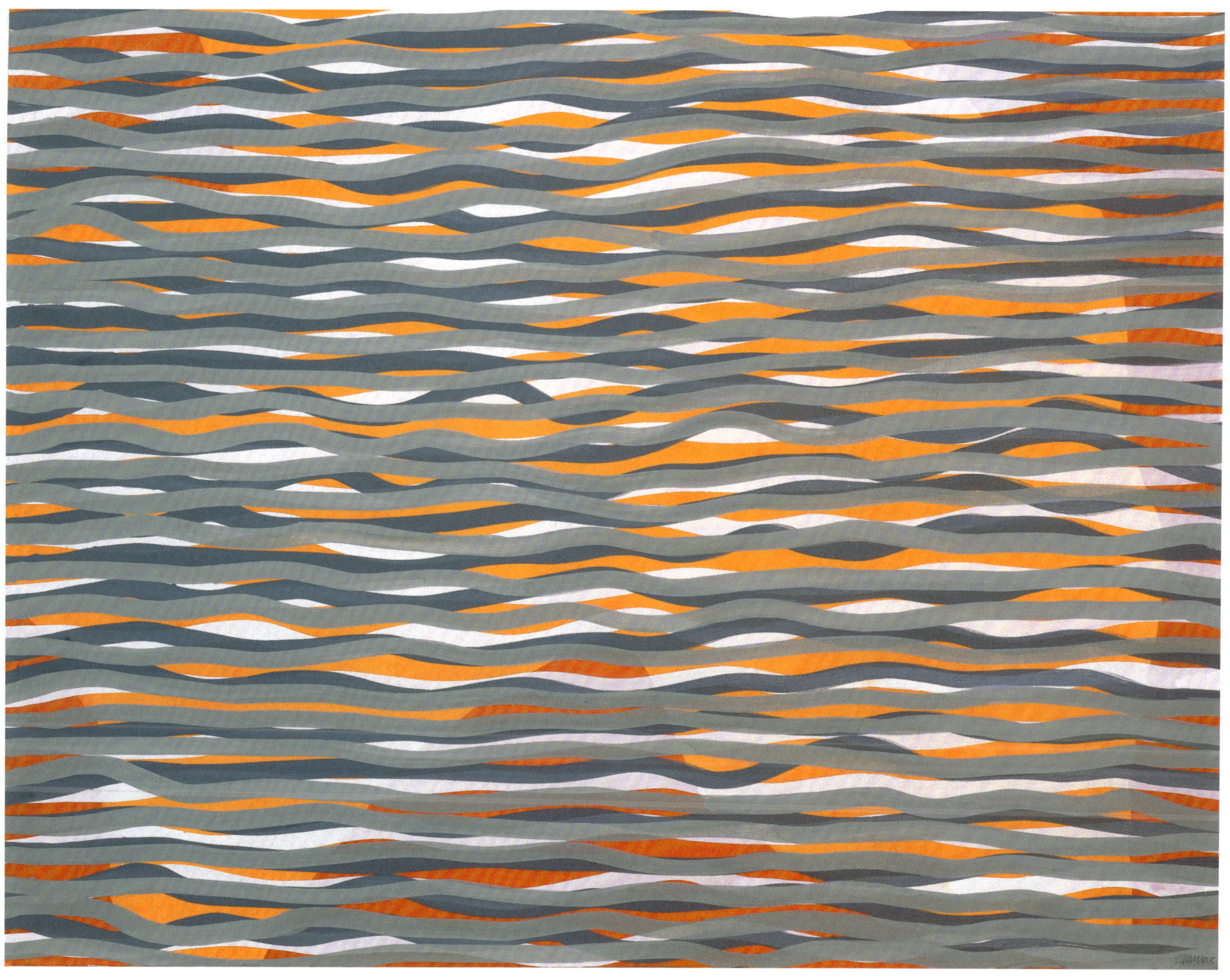

WALL DRAWING #896 COLORS/CURVES 1999
Lascaux acrylic paint
First drawn by Sachiko Cho, Mark Dickey, John Hogan, Aron Murkis, Hidemi Nomura, Jeff Pook, Emily Ripley, Anthony Sansotta, Todd Weinstein
First installation Christie's, New York
Room 29 ½ × 48 × 18 feet
Collection Christie's, New York, New York

Photographed at Christie's, New York

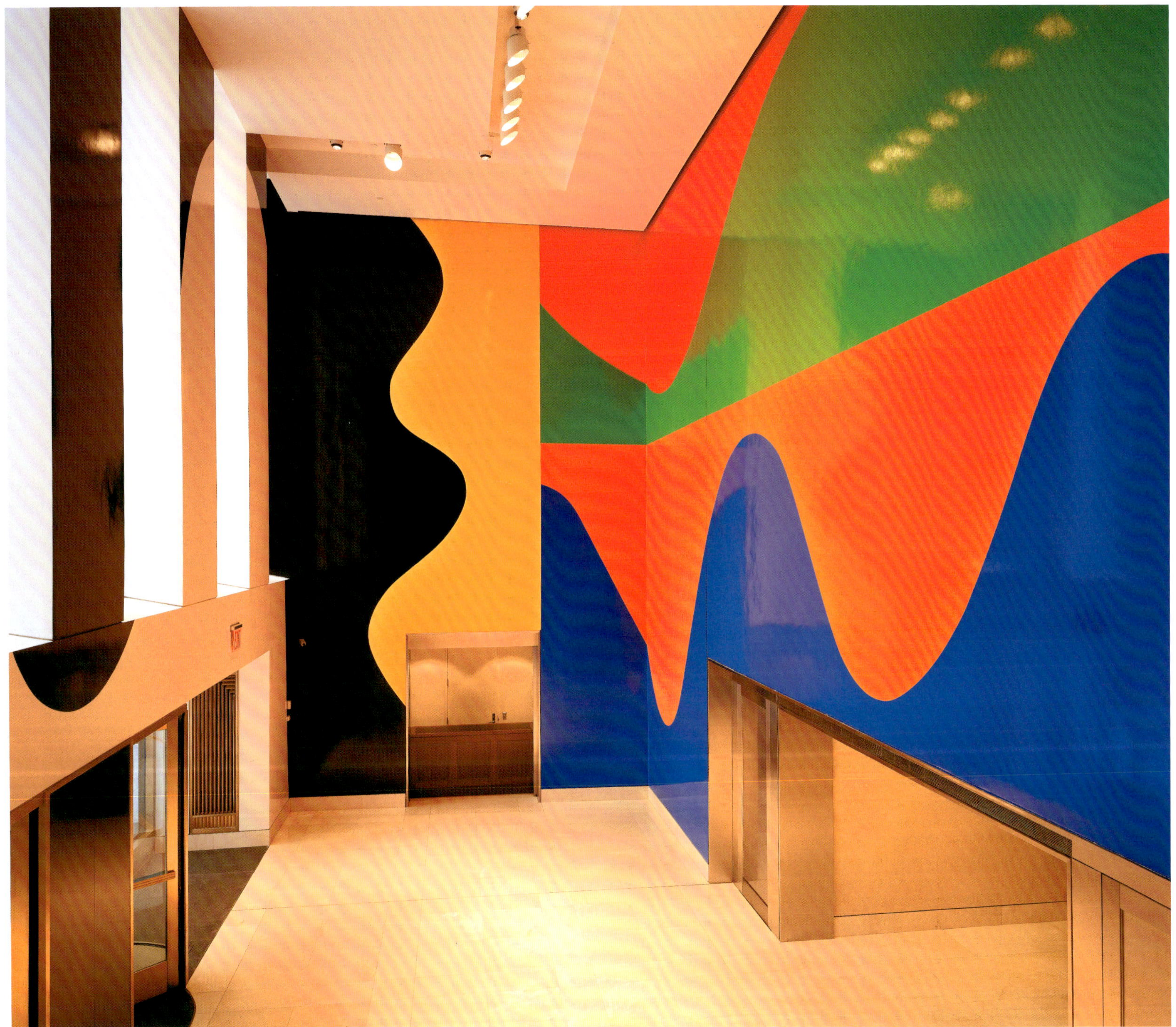

SPLOTCH #20 2006
Fiberglass
68 x 68 x 68 inches

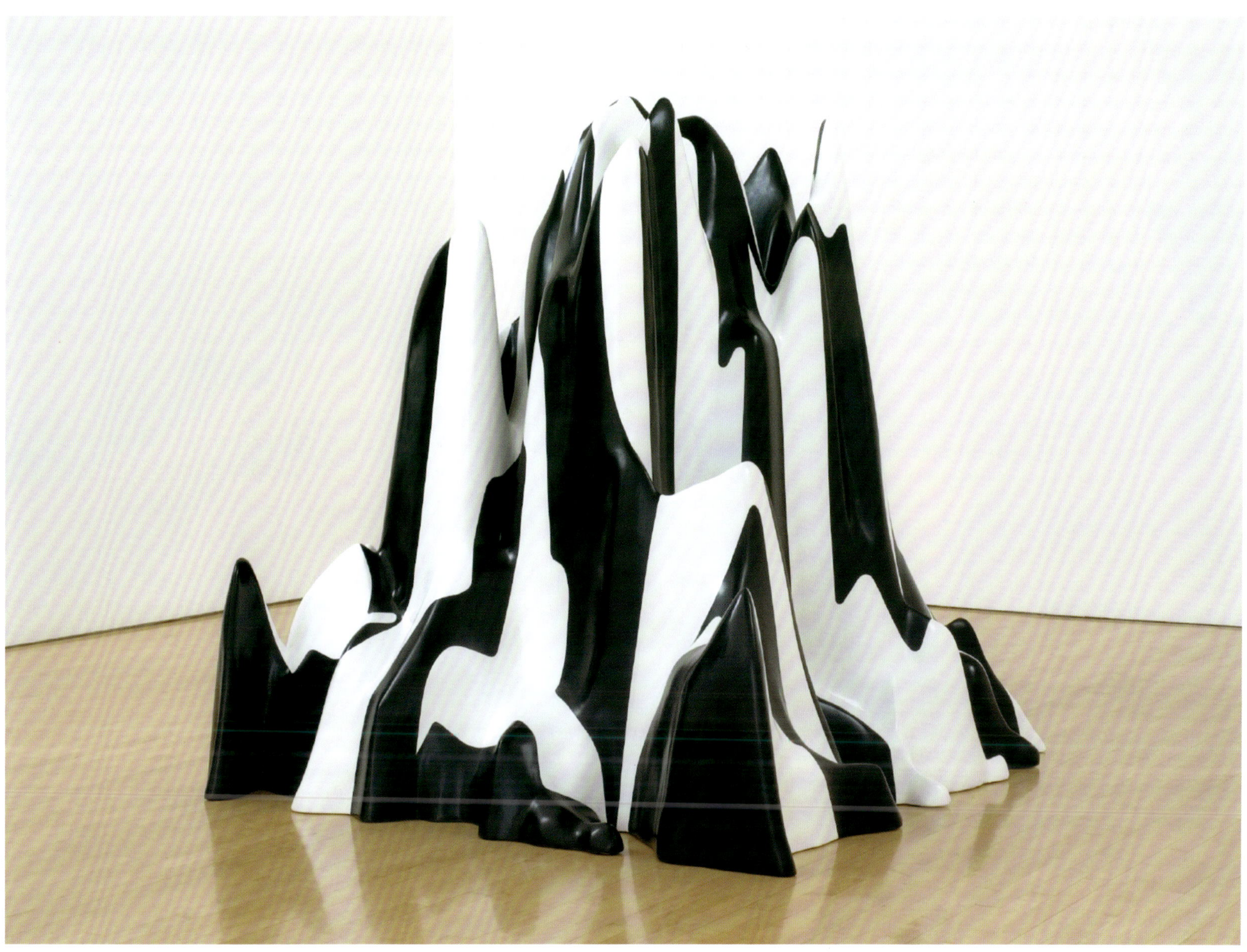

A *Splotch* begins with LeWitt's sketch of a "footprint'" or view of the form from above. Based on this, his fabricator, Yoshitsugu Nakama, generates with the help of a computer program a three-dimensional image from which a structure is made of construction foam. Sanded and coated with epoxy resin, the form is then finished with acrylic paint. The apparently free-form, random appearance of the *Splotches* is a surprising contrast to the controlled geometry of the earlier structures, but the dimensions of the *Splotch* in the exhibition may suggest otherwise. Height, width, and depth are identical, as in a cube.

In 2005, LeWitt inaugurated a series of "scribble" wall drawings, in which countless tiny, irregular pencil lines are scrawled on a wall surface. The areas where the lines are more densely overlaid

SCRIBBLES 2005
Pencil on paper
22 ½ × 30 inches

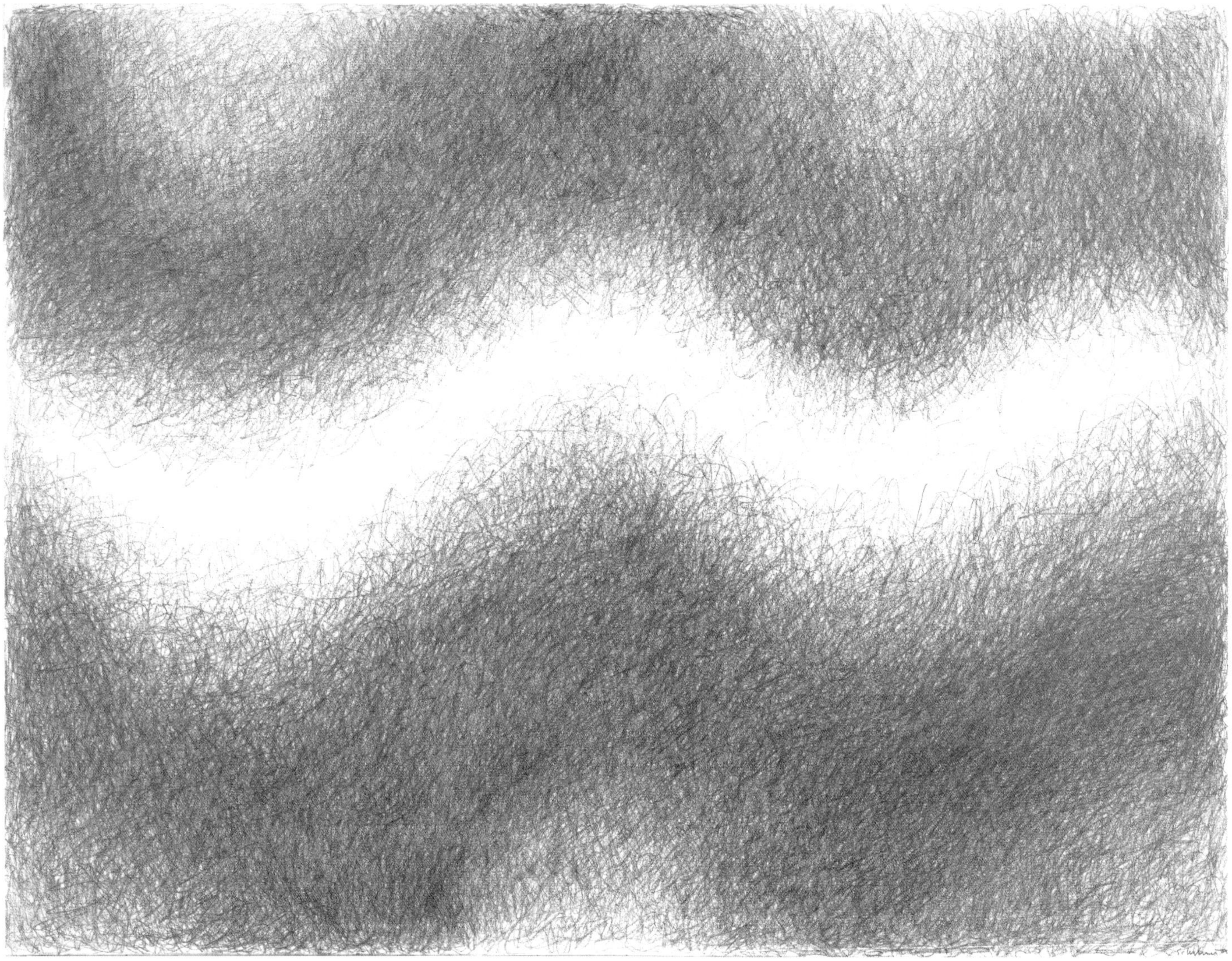

are the darkest parts of the image, and the white wall emerges where there are no pencil marks. Such a chiaroscuro effect was also a salient feature of the hatching in the early drawings, in which the intersection of straight lines resulted in shaded areas. LeWitt has recently made drawings on paper that explore various configurations of scribbled lines, yet another example of his simultaneous development of an idea in several media.

LeWitt's art has expanded and flourished in ways that might have been difficult to predict from his work of forty years ago. The introduction of rich color in the 1980s, the appearance of irregular form and its recent incarnation in the *Splotches*, his redefining of drawing in the *Scribbles*, all have been surprising, yet clearly are part of a unified vision.

CIRCLE WITH TOWERS 2005
2,230 concrete blocks
Overall 14 × 25 × 25 feet; each block 8 × 8 × 8 inches
Installation Madison Square Park, New York, 2005

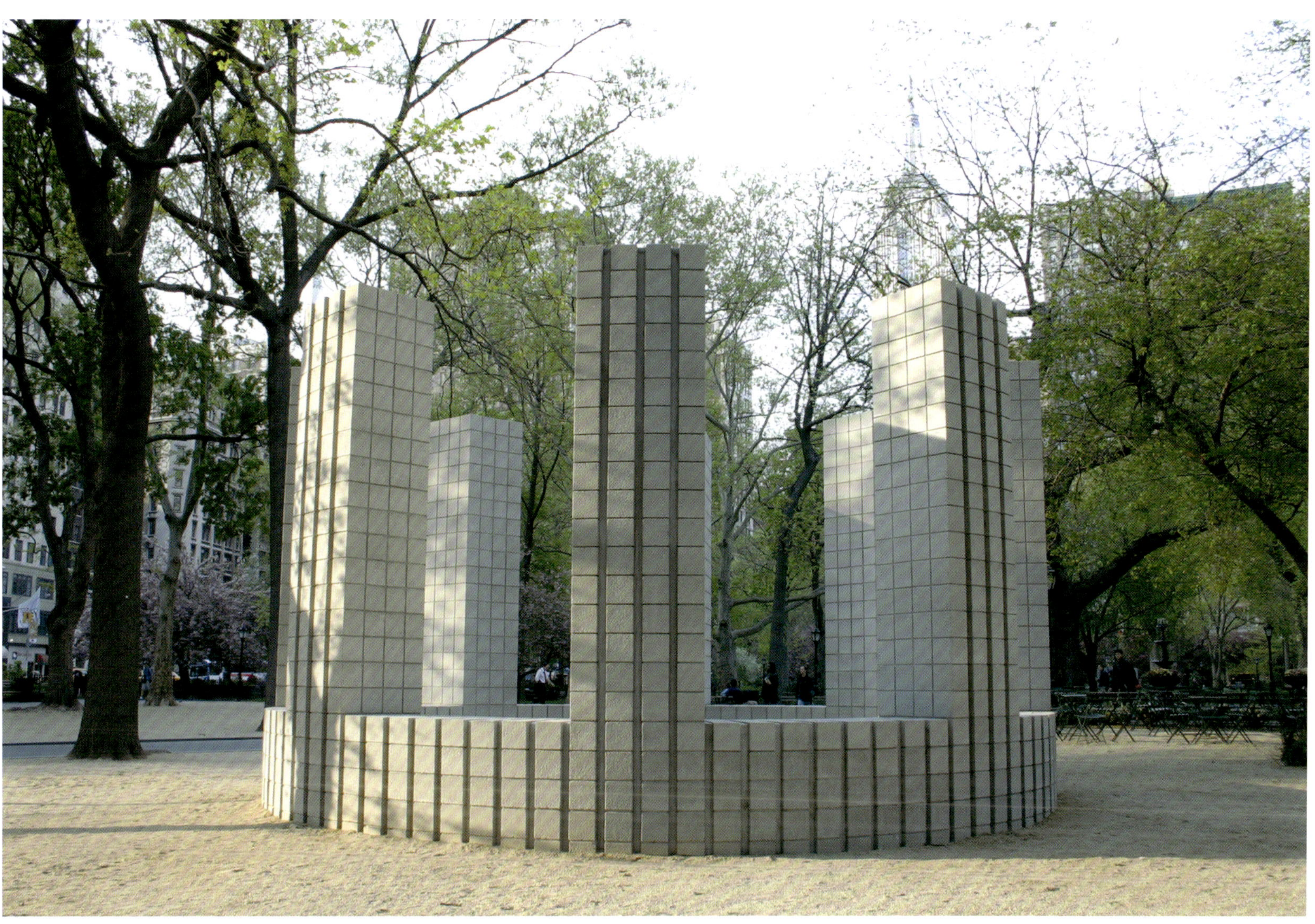

1. Andrea Miller-Keller, "Excerpts from a Correspondence 1981–83," in Susanna Singer et al., *Sol LeWitt Wall Drawings 1968–84* (Amsterdam: Stedelijk Museum 1984), 21.
2. Lucy Lippard, *Six Years: The Dematerialization of the Art Object from 1966 to 1972* (1973; reprint, Berkeley and Los Angeles: University of California Press 1997), viii.
3. Camilla Gray, *The Great Experiment: Russian Art 1863–1922* (New York: Harry N. Abrams 1962).
4. "Paragraphs On Conceptual Art," *Artforum* 5, no. 10 (June 1967), 79–83; "Sentences On Conceptual Art," *Art-Language* 1, no. 1 (May 1969) 11–13.
5. The Xerox Book, or *Carl Andre, Robert Barry, Douglas Huebler, Joseph Kosuth, Sol LeWitt, Robert Morris, Lawrence Weiner* (New York: Seth Siegelaub and John W. Wendler, [December] 1968).
6. Lippard, *Six Years*, vii.

Robert Ryman (American, b. 1930)
Untitled 1964
Oil on linen
7 ½ × 7 ½ inches

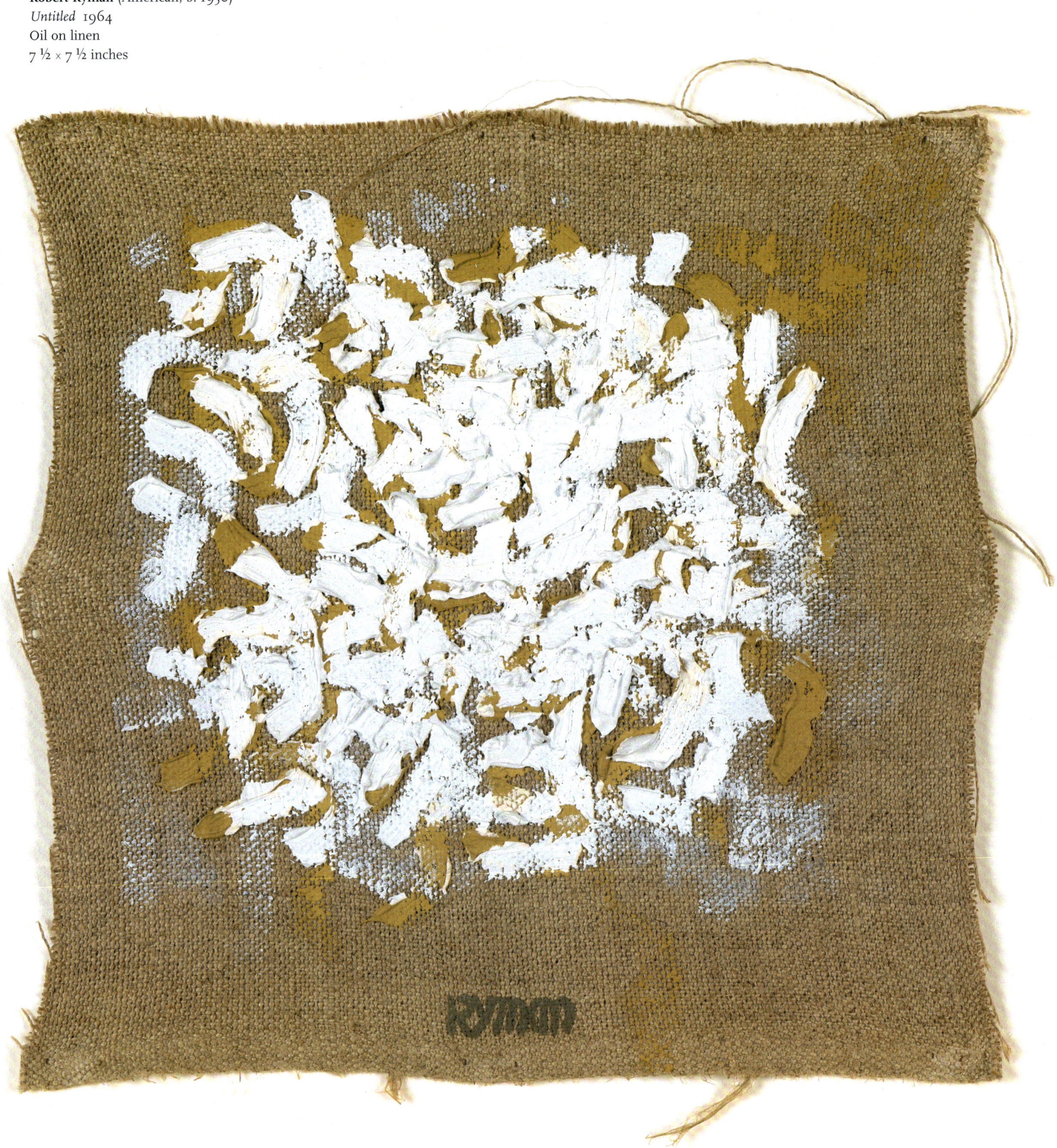

THE LEWITT COLLECTION

Dean Swanson

I first visited Chester, Connecticut, in 2003. Sol and Carol LeWitt have lived in this small New England town since the late 1980s in a handsome Federal-style house. The nearby studio building has a spectacular view of surrounding woodland. Prior to my visit, Janet Passehl, curator and registrar of the LeWitt Collection, had provided me with a list of works the artist and his wife have assembled, an impressive group of paintings, sculptures, drawings, prints, photographs, and books by 750 artists. The collection is housed in a warehouse building in Chester, in conditions worthy of an up-to-date museum—climate control, rolling storage walls, sheets of acid-free paper separating unframed works.

LeWitt's own work that he has retained from over forty years of his production are also stored here. Although the collection comprises such disparate objects as eighteenth-century Japanese prints, serial locomotion studies by the nineteenth-century Anglo-American photographer Eadweard Muybridge, and early-twentieth-century furniture by the Dutch designer Gerrit Rietveld, these fall outside the time during which LeWitt has made and collected art. *LeWitt x 2* focuses on the period between 1960 and the present.

The challenge of selecting an exhibition from thousands of works became easier when I learned that some of the collection was on view that summer at the nearby New Britain Museum of American Art, and that show had been curated by Sol LeWitt himself. Many of the works shown in New Britain are included in the present, larger exhibition. I have added artists to the roster in order to represent the scope and character of the collection, and Sol made some excellent suggestions for alternates and additions to my initial selections.

During that first visit to Chester, as I talked with Sol and Carol about the collection, I came to appreciate the diversity and historical significance of this extraordinary repository of art of the past half-century. While the LeWitt Collection resembles a museum's holdings in its size, it is unmistakably an expression of the LeWitts' personal connections with the artists who made the works. Museum collections represent styles and movements in their historical context, a mandate that affects acquisition choices. Private collectors typically have wish lists of artists, even specific works, that they seek out. Corporate collections are frequently managed by curators who pursue a particular direction, sometimes with a view to providing decoration for company offices and public spaces. What sets the LeWitt Collection apart is the manner in which much of the art has been acquired. With the exception of some purchases and gifts, most of the works were exchanged for works by Sol LeWitt. The formation of the collection has been driven by the associations and friendships the LeWitts have made with artists. Artists have occasionally responded to a proposed exchange by offering a choice of works, but, in Carol LeWitt's words, "Typically, we don't choose."[1]

Sol LeWitt began trading art with his fellow artists in the early 1960s. In his circle of friends, exchanging ideas often led to an exchange of work. Among the first pieces to enter the collection are paintings by two of LeWitt's former coworkers at the Museum of Modern Art. Robert Mangold's small monochromatic painting is neither symbolic nor associative in the way that Abstract Expressionistic painting had been. In a painting made around the same time, Robert Ryman daubed paint at the center of a piece of linen whose irregular edges are unpainted, thus calling attention to the materiality of both the paint and the ground. The white paint contrasts with the texture of the raw linen, and the central placement of the brushmarks allows no hierarchical relationships between compositional elements.

Among the works in the LeWitt Collection that represent the Minimalist esthetic of the 1960s is a series of small paintings on paper by Jo Baer. These share a format based on edges treated similarly but in subtly varied colors. The central area, traditionally the focus of visual activity in paintings, is left empty.

Donald Judd's articles and reviews, which began to appear in 1959 in *Arts Magazine*, advocated an art of simple forms and unmodulated, "anonymous" surfaces. He deplored the gestural painting of the Abstract Expressionists for its illusionism and emotional content. When he began to show his own work in 1963, it was three-dimensional, something between painting and sculpture. By the mid-1960s, Judd was having his objects industrially fabricated in order to eliminate the visual distraction of craftsmanship. The wall-mounted piece in the LeWitt collection has a smooth, lacquered finish that focuses attention on the progression of forms across the wall. It alludes to nothing outside the work. Judd called works like this "specific objects."

One of Sol LeWitt's closest friends was the artist Eva Hesse. *Accession V* (1967) is one of the few pieces she made with fabricated parts. In a regular pattern of holes in a manufactured galvanized steel box Hesse again and again painstakingly threaded a short length of rubber tubing through two adjacent holes. The resulting tactile interior questions the industrial Minimalist cube. The ambiguous, organic references of the work effectively subvert the carefully ordered rows. *Accession V* is one of more than a dozen important examples of Hesse's work in the LeWitt Collection.

Conceptualism is a term applied to art that is based on ideas, in which only secondary importance is accorded the visible form it takes. In contrast to the formal purity of Minimalist works, an art of ideas signaled a shift of emphasis from objects to information. A key text by a leading critic of the previous generation, Clement Greenberg's 1961 book *Art and Culture*, is concerned with how art looks, with an art that is purely visual and from which all external references have been excluded. But for some artists, art that is merely good to look at was a dead end. Sol LeWitt articulated an alternative program when he published "Paragraphs on Conceptual Art" in 1967 and "Sentences on Conceptual Art" in 1969. His clear, practical observations on the nature of idea-driven art argue that "ideas alone can be works of art."

Among the major figures associated with early conceptual art are John Baldessari, Robert Barry, Dan Graham, Douglas Huebler, and Joseph Kosuth. These artists were LeWitt's friends, and they traded works with him throughout the 1960s and '70s. As a result, the LeWitt Collection is a unique, personal record of the birth of a movement..

Donald Judd (American, 1928–1994)
Untitled 1965
Painted steel
5 × 68 × 8 ½ inches

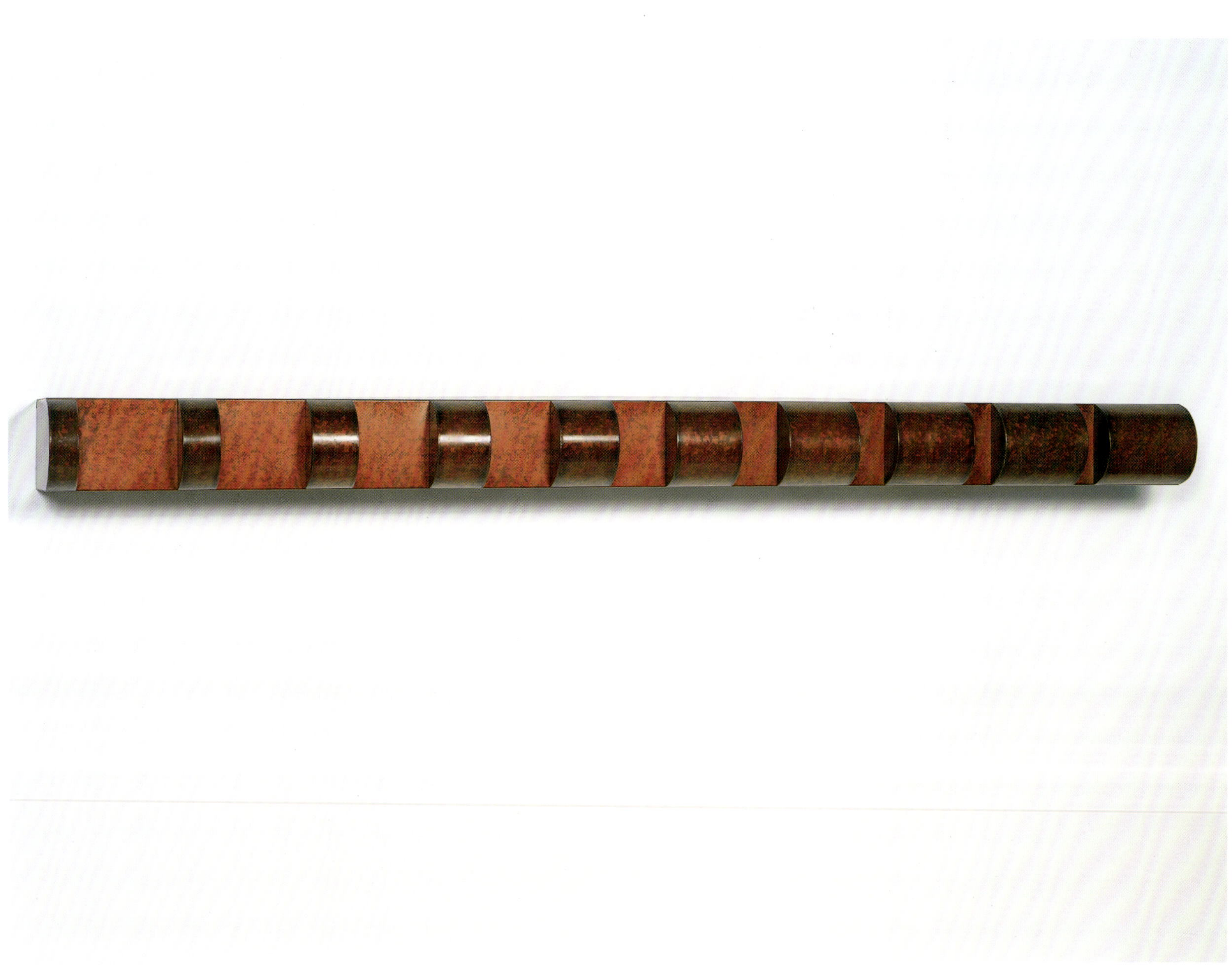

Eva Hesse (American, b. Germany, 1926–1970)
Accession V 1967
Galvanized steel, rubber tubing
10 × 10 × 10 inches

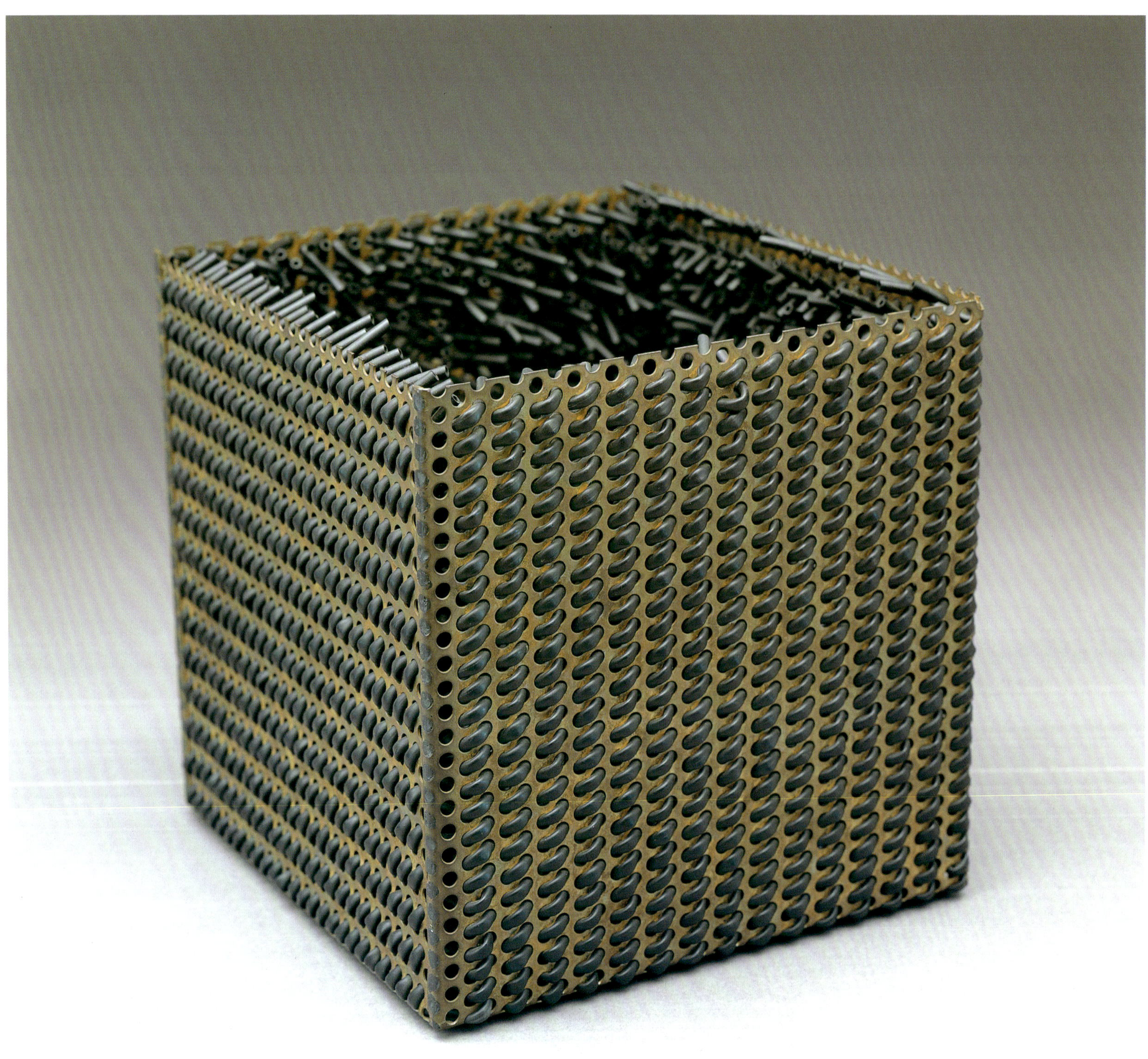

Hans Haacke (American, b. Germany, 1936)
Condensation Cube 1963–65
Water in Plexiglas box
10 × 10 × 10 inches

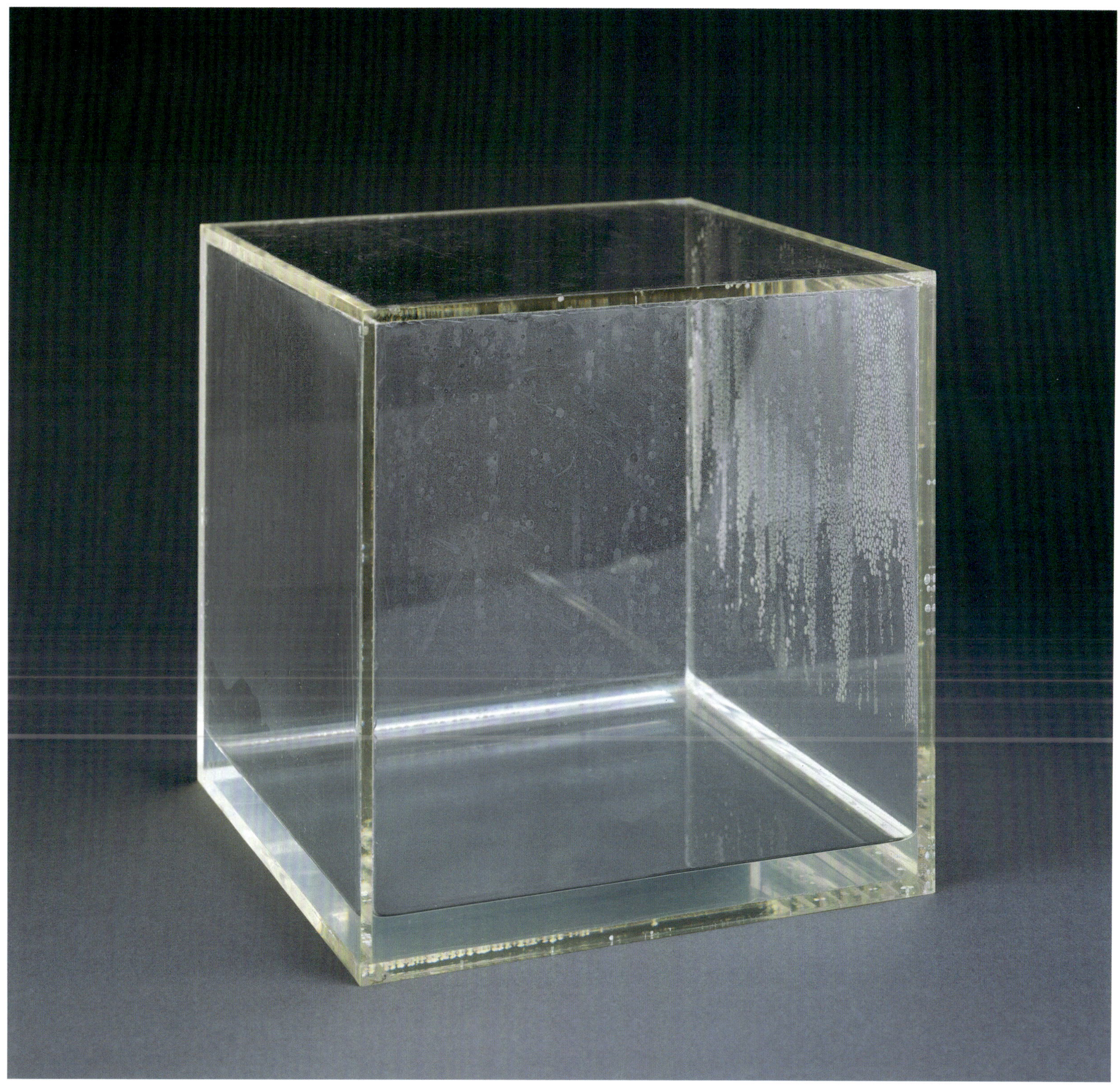

Hanne Darboven (German, b. 1941)
Zeichnung (Drawing) 1968
Ink on paper
39 ½ × 27 ½ inches

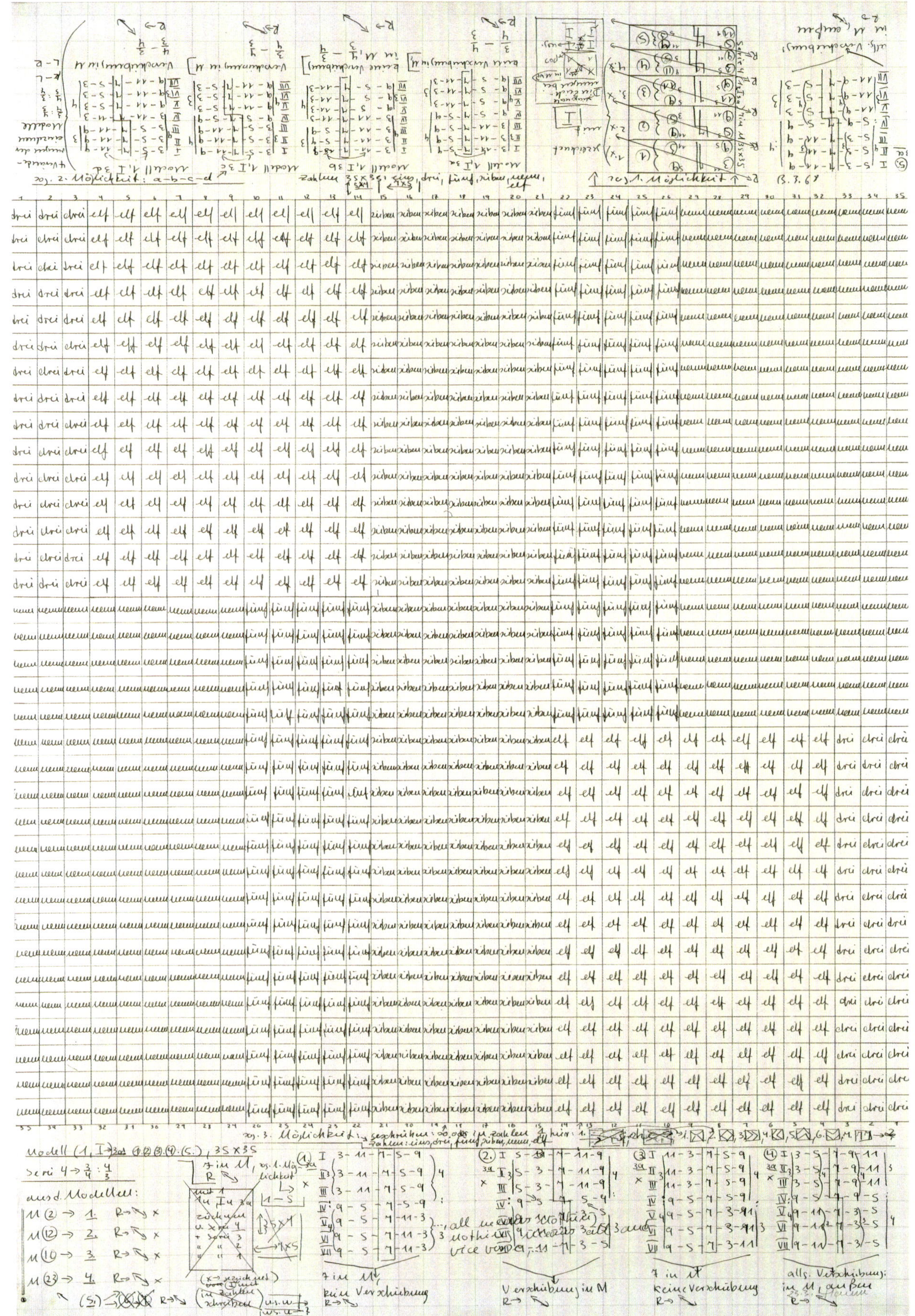

Processes and systems are the focus of much conceptual art. Hans Haacke's *Condensation Cube* is one of several water boxes he made in the mid-1960s, sculptures that react to the physical environment. At first glance, the simple Plexiglas cube looks like an elemental Minimalist form. Look again: the interior of the box is clouded with vapor, which is set in action by the temperature of the gallery. Haacke has said that the cube "merges with the environment in a relationship that is better understood as a 'system' of interdependent processes."[2]

The German artist Hanne Darboven lived in New York for several years in the mid-1960s. A close friend of LeWitt, Darboven has made art that consists of her handwriting. In works such as *Zeichnung (Drawing)*, she selected a series of numbers and proceeded to cover a grid of squares with German words for the numbers, obsessively repeating the words in rows across the paper. The writing process was the impetus for the work.

Much conceptual art is language based, as exemplified by the work of On Kawara. He has marked the passage of time and the events of his life in various ways that can be considered documents of his existence. He once mailed a long series of daily postcards that stated the time he got up. Among his best-known works are paintings such as the one in this exhibition, which consists of a date on a solid color background. This painting marks the date he met Sol LeWitt: May 22, 1967.

The proliferation of art periodicals in the 1960s, along with the development of photocopying technology, undoubtedly encouraged the use of texts and photographic images in conceptual works. John Baldessari's *Ingres and Other Parables* is a set of panels that incorporate photographs with photocopied typewritten texts. Each text is a narrative about an art-related subject that concludes with a moral.

In an iconic work called *Homes for America*, Dan Graham parodied a home magazine feature using photographs of housing developments in New Jersey accompanied by a text. One of Graham's images depicts row houses in Bayonne. The banal, repetitive tract dwellings resemble the serial forms of a Minimalist sculpture, a wry critique on Graham's part.

While all this activity was going on in New York, artists in other parts of the world were making art that shared some the same conceptualist themes and attitudes. In 1969, an exhibition at the Kunsthalle in Düsseldorf, Germany, called *Prospect 69* included the art of the Americans LeWitt, Ryman, and Robert Smithson, alongside that of Darboven, the German-born Haacke, the Dutch-born Jan Dibbets, the British Richard Long, several Italians of the Arte Povera group, and the German husband-and-wife team Bernd and Hilla Becher. LeWitt had shown at the Konrad Fischer Gallery in Düsseldorf two years before, and was already acquainted with some of the other artists included in *Prospect 69*. They had begun to exchange work, and the LeWitt Collection took on an increasingly international character.

The term *Arte Povera*, which translates approximately as "impoverished art," was coined by the Italian critic Germano Celant to describe the work by certain artists in Turin, Milan, Genoa, and Rome in the 1960s. More overtly sociopolitical in their goals than their American and British contemporaries, the Italian artists rejected advanced consumer culture and frequently referred in their work to a preindustrial, even primitive, past. Lacking faith in technological "progress," they used "poor" materials not customarily associated with art.

The emphasis on materials in Arte Povera contrasts with the increasing tendency toward dematerialization in American conceptual art of the era. While artists in New York were producing Xeroxed documents in ring binders, some of the more sensational Arte Povera works consisted of a huge pile of rags heaped around a gilded plaster cast of a classical statue (Michelangelo Pistoletto) and live horses loosed in an interior exhibition space (Jannis Kounellis).

The LeWitt Collection includes numerous works by the artists associated with the Arte Povera movement. Giulio Paolini is represented in this exhibition by an installation of tacks that radiate out over the wall around a box filled with similar tacks. Mario Merz is best known for a series of sculptures that refer to igloo forms, round shapes that recall dwellings of ancient societies. Merz has used a similar circular configuration in his floor sculpture included here, a form without a beginning or an end.

Alighiero Boetti became associated with the Arte Povera circle in the late 1960s. A decade later he began to make his well-known maps of the world, executed in brilliant colors by women embroiderers in Afghanistan and Pakistan. This pre-industrial way of producing an image was the medium Boetti chose for the work in this exhibition, a giant embroidered tribute in honor of Sol LeWitt's sixtieth birthday.

The expansion of the collection in the 1970s mirrors LeWitt's increasing number of contacts with artists abroad as his wall drawings were made in numerous venues and his work

On Kawara (Japanese, b. 1933)
May 22, 1967 1967
Acrylic on canvas
10 × 13 inches

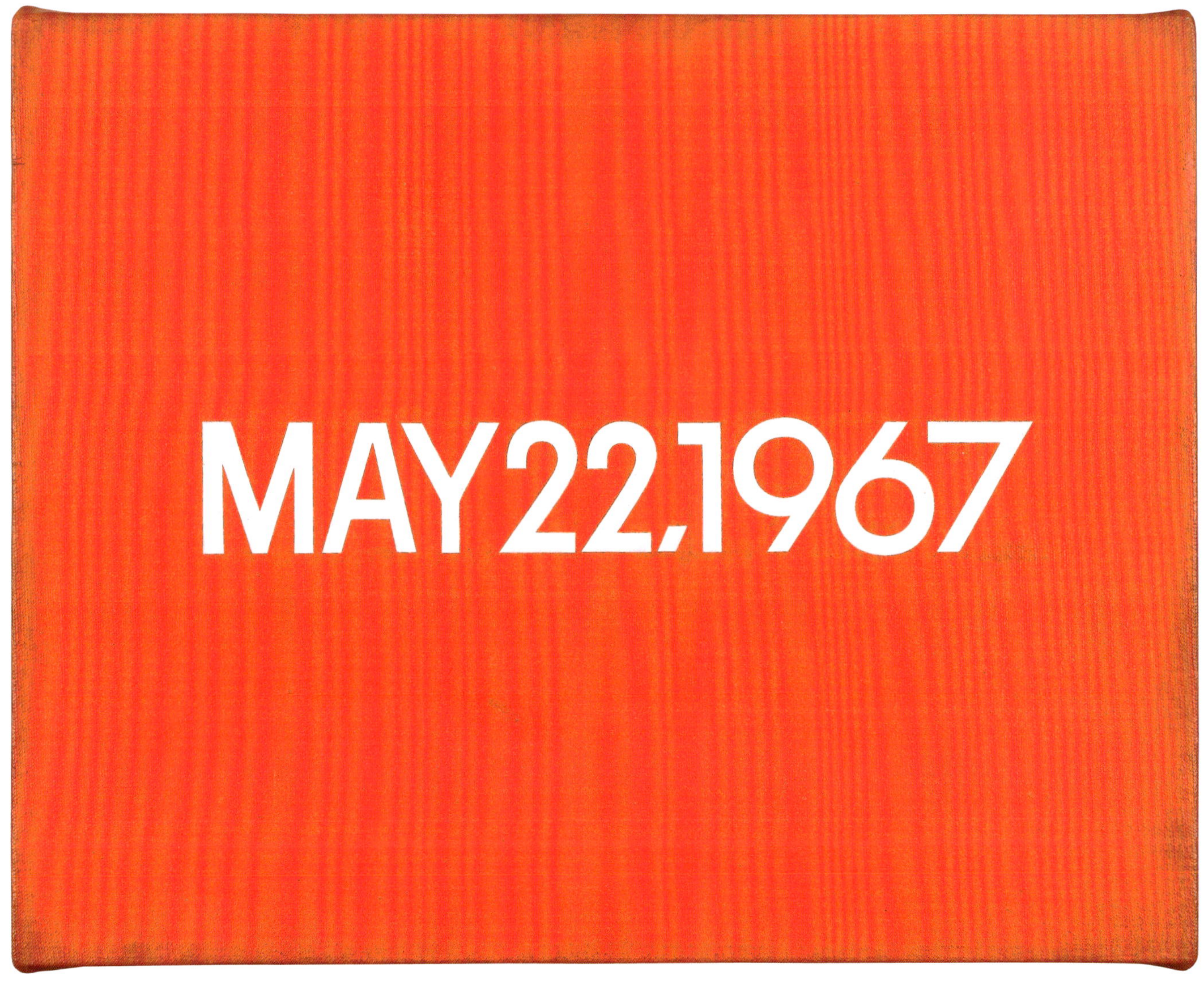

John Baldessari (American, b. 1931)
The Great Artist, from the suite *Ingres and Other Parables* 1971
Black-and-white photograph with photocopy
12 ¾ x 20 ¾ inches

THE GREAT ARTIST

Once there was an artist that believed in other artists. That is, he knew that one day a Great Artist would come with the answer to art. Our artist was adequate but not great, as were most other artists that he knew. And the answer could only come from a Great Artist.

One afternoon all the artists in the bar were talking about a new artist in town - a Great Colorist. Could this artist be the Great Artist, our artist thought. Excitedly he studied every brush stroke of the Colorist. What blues! What reds! What daring! Every painting by the Colorist seemed right.

Months later, while looking at a painting of the Colorist, a blue next to a red didn't seem to sing. Something was wrong. Sadly the artist knew that the Great Artist hadn't arrived, and he went back to his own painting and to waiting.

Years after, the art magazines spoke of the Great Emancipator who had freed painting. Art would never be the same. "Brilliant, incisive strategy," read the magazine article. And it was true - the Emancipator had indeed freed art, and our friend's art work took on new meaning as did the work of many other artists he knew.

Art sang with freedom. But soon every artist was free and also the same, and our artist again knew the Great Artist hadn't come. He went back to work and to waiting.

While attending a lecture on art one night, our artist heard the speaker mention a new artist unheard of by all but a few - The Great Philosopher. The Philosopher was not deceived by the outward appearance of art. He understood the underlying structure behind all art past and present - a secret that explained all of human communication. Surely at last, this must be the Great Artist. Our artist listened and learned. "Don't be fooled by how art looks since art is really in the mind as an idea," he was told.

And our artist wasn't fooled. At least not for a long while. Then something seemed wrong again and he went back to work, and to waiting.

Moral: Art is where you find it.

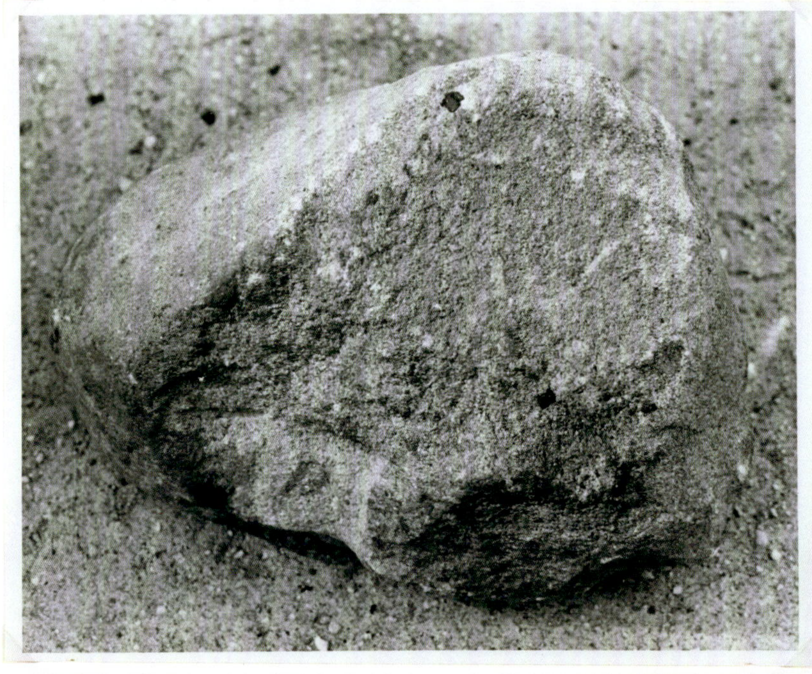

Dan Graham (American, b. 1942)
Row Houses, Bayonne, New Jersey, from the series *Homes for America* 1966
Color photograph
11 × 14 inches

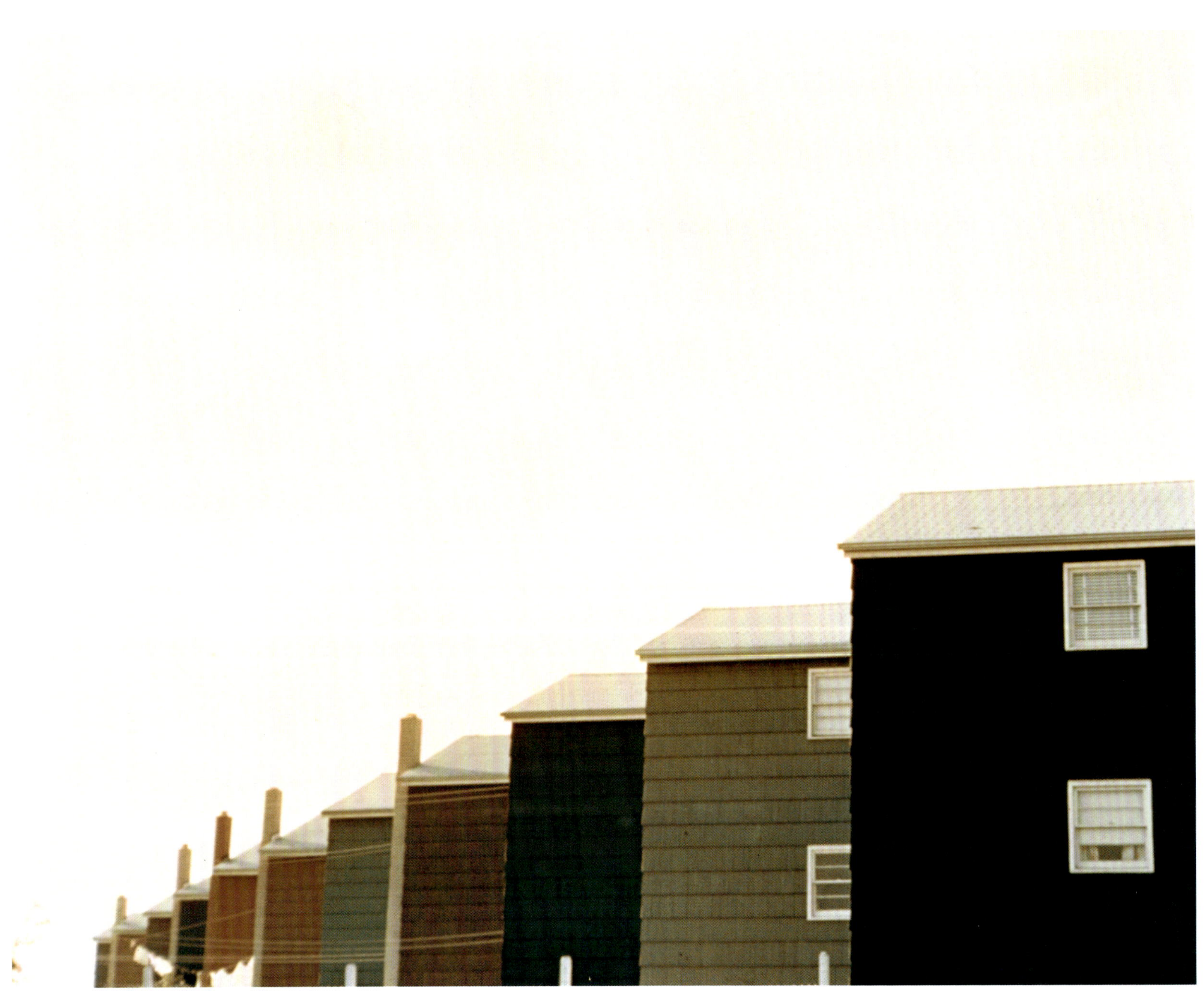

Mario Merz (Italian, 1925–2003)
(Without Title) 1983
Metal tubing, sheet metal, and paint
8 inches × 95 inches (diameter)

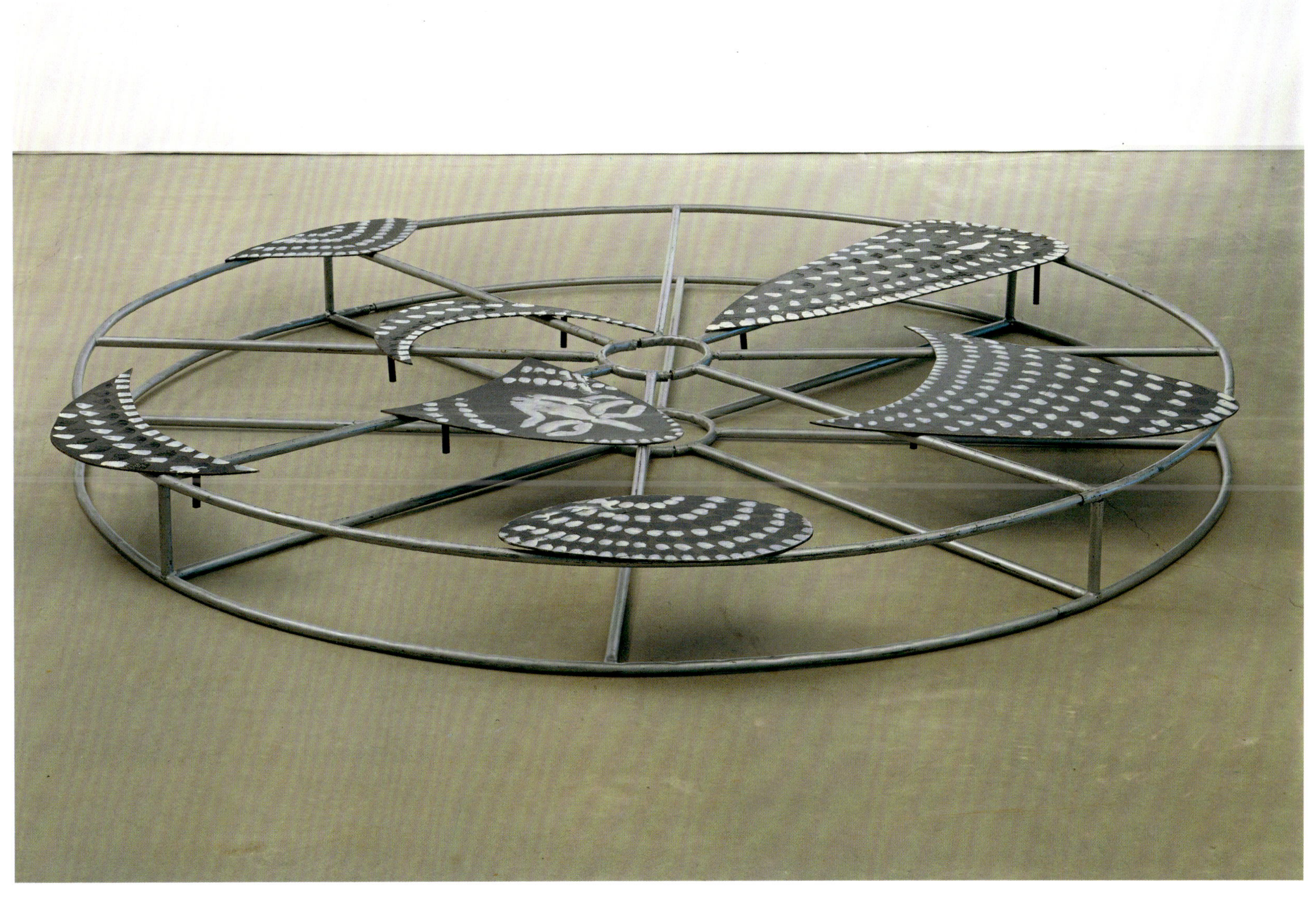

Alighiero Boetti (Italian, 1940–1994)
Untitled 1988
Embroidery, ballpoint ink, marker, and pencil on canvas
57 × 55 inches

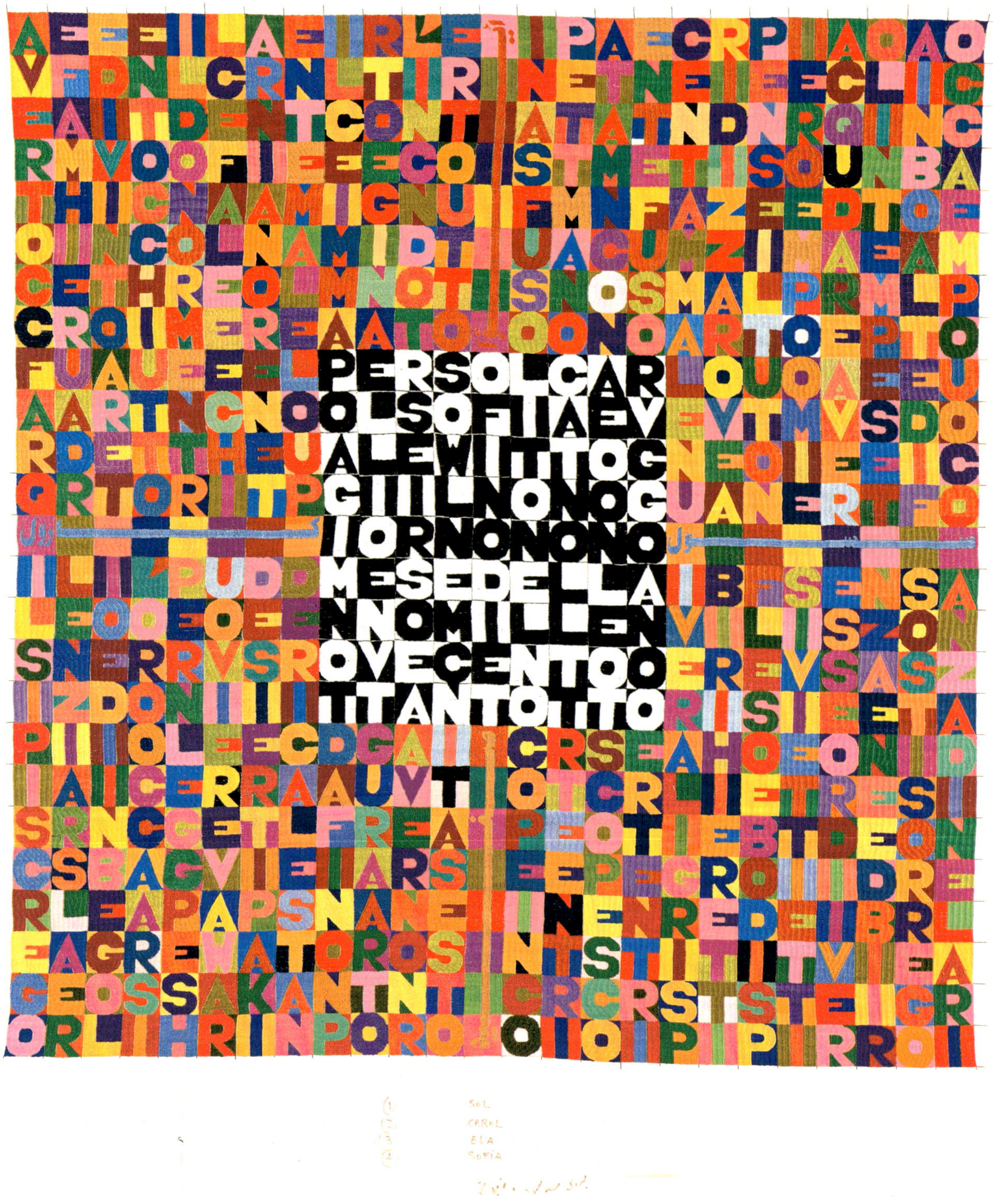

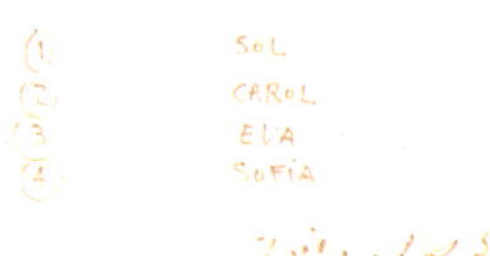

was the subject of many exhibitions. Following the 1982 marriage of Sol LeWitt and Carol Androccio, for several years the couple's primary residence was their house in Spoleto, Italy. Acquisitions during the 1980s increasingly reflected their European contacts, while American works continued to be added. The pattern LeWitt had established of exchanging works continued even as he bought more art. Early in our conversations, he identified several areas of concentration in the collection. Conceptual art of the 1960s and '70s is clearly one of these. Other strengths include sculpture and photography.

The sculptures in this exhibition represent a multitude of styles, and in media range from the traditional cast bronze used by Juan Muñoz in the compelling *Double Lamp* to the muslin and buttons of Janet Passehl's suspended piece, which can be read as a metaphor for a garment. Other works refer to the human figure (Robin Heidi Kennedy's *Seated Red Mother*) and to architectural forms (Franco Dellerba's *Islam 1*).

Jackie Ferrara, in a 1992 interview, said that Sol LeWitt "was the first one to buy my work . . . three sculptures and a drawing." Ferrara further related that the pieces were in LeWitt's studio when a gallerist visited, and "that is how Max Protetch became my dealer for many years."[3] In *A-126 B Pyramid*, Ferrara built up layers of wood in a shape that references ancient architecture, yet the elemental geometric form also relates to pared-down contemporaneous works, which were typically made of sleek industrial materials. By executing the sculpture in wood, with all its textural irregularities, the artist subverts the Minimalist context.

Born after the end of World War II, the Austrian sculptor Franz West began his career in the 1970s, following the heyday of the Vienna Actionist movement. The ritualistic actions of that performance group profoundly affected the work of many young artists, and their influence can be seen in West's funky, anti-formalist sculptures. West often stayed in the LeWitt's Essex Street loft in the late 1980s. After each visit, he would leave a piece as a gift. The papier-mâché sphere in the exhibition is one of five works by West in the LeWitt Collection.

Siah Armajani, who came to the United States as a young man from his native Iran, became fascinated with early American structures such as barns, one-room schoolhouses, and covered bridges. He applied the traditional techniques used to construct buildings in his first bridge sculptures. Some were models, not intended to be built in full scale. In the piece exhibited here, Armajani refers to the numerical system discovered by the Italian mathematician Leonardo Pisano Fibonacci in the thirteenth century, in which each number in the sequence is the sum of the two numbers that precede it (1,1,2,3,5, and so on). In this bridge model, the vertical members of the bridge are spaced at intervals reflecting this sequential relationship.

LeWitt first became acquainted with the work of the turn-of-the-twentieth-century photographer Eadweard Muybridge in the 1950s. The sequential images in the Muybridge motion studies of human and animals influenced his own thinking about serial imagery. In addition, LeWitt has created several important photographic works, including *Photogrids* (1977) and the 1980 *Autobiography*, in which he recorded in great detail the contents of his Hester Street loft. Those images, each 2 ⅝ inches square, are arranged nine to a page. They document windows, walls, furniture, tools, plants, kitchen and bathroom accoutrements, clothing, books, and more. The cumulative effect of a page, and the totality of pages, is a fascinating record of the artist's life.

The early 1960s, when LeWitt began collecting, was also a time of growing interest in photography on the part of artists. For conceptual artists, the medium represented a means of conveying information. Richard Long, Hamish Fulton, and Thomas Joshua Cooper recorded with the camera processes and activities such as the effects of their own presence on the landscape. Other conceptual artists used cheap cameras and amateur snapshot techniques to reinforce a "just the facts" attitude about information. Ironically, in the wake of the deliberate amateurism of the conceptualists, serious art photography was re-evaluated. As late as 1960, the work of well-known photographers brought low prices compared with work in other media. In 1995, photographer Jeff Wall wrote that "photoconceptualism led the way toward the complete acceptance of photography as art."[4]

One of the factors that created an increased awareness of photography's potential was the inclusion in important international exhibitions of Bernd and Hilla Becher's work. Only after their photographs were shown in the groundbreaking *Information* exhibition at New York's Museum of Modern Art in 1970 were the Bechers claimed as conceptual artists. They did not consider themselves to be so. Their self-appointed mission was to photograph various kinds of industrial buildings—cooling towers, blast furnaces, grain silos, lime kilns—and to collect the images as an act of archival documentation. Traveling about, the Bechers photographed the structures uniformly and objectively in black and white, without shadows and unpeopled. They then arranged beautiful prints of the resulting high-quality images in series and grids. The parallel

Jackie Ferrara (American, b. 1929)
A-126 B Pyramid 1974
Wood (Novaply)
27 ½ × 27 ¼ × 27 ¼ inches

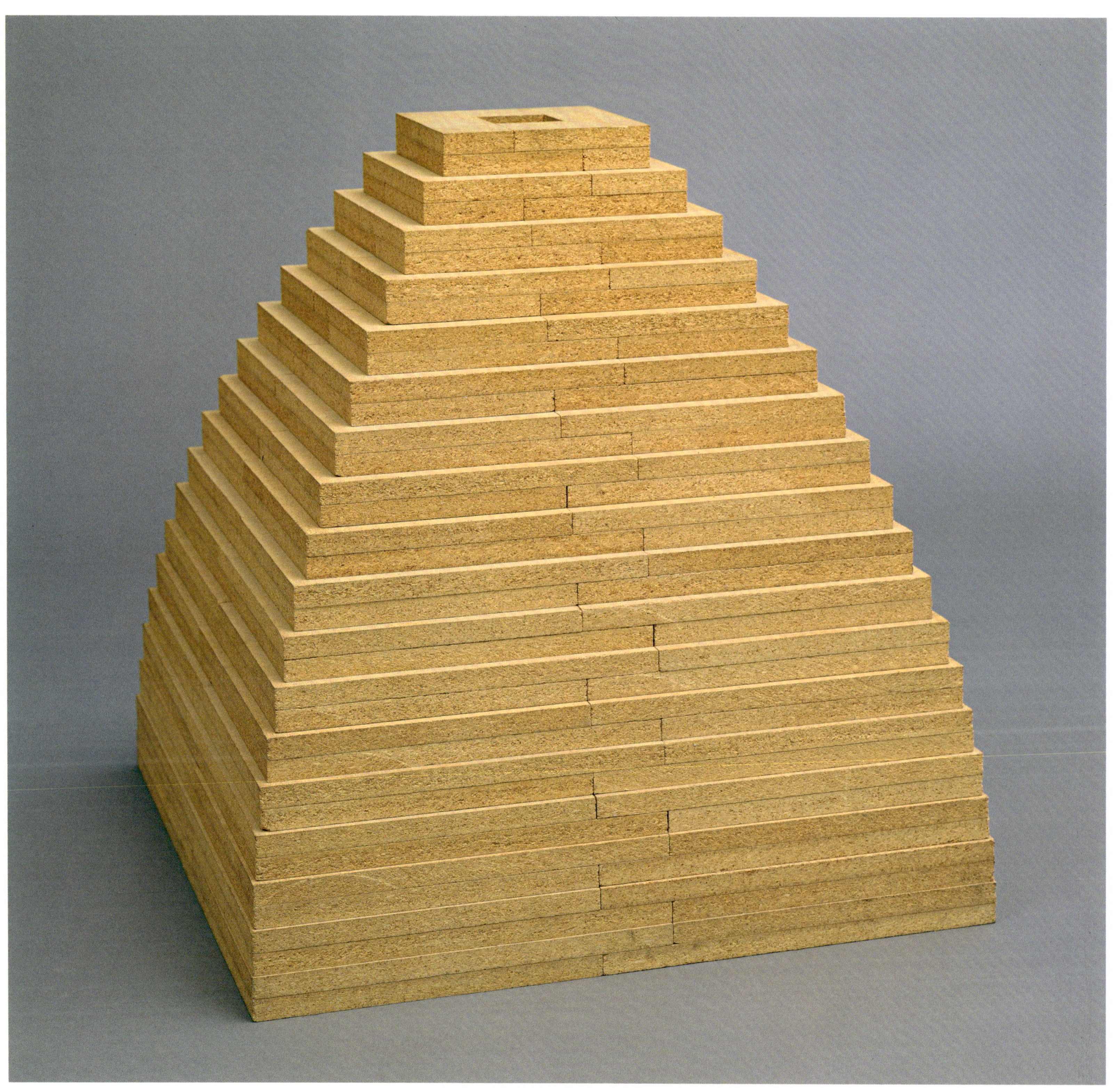

Franz West (Austrian, b. 1947)
Untitled (Sphairos) 1988
Painted papier-mâché
15 × 14 × 20 inches

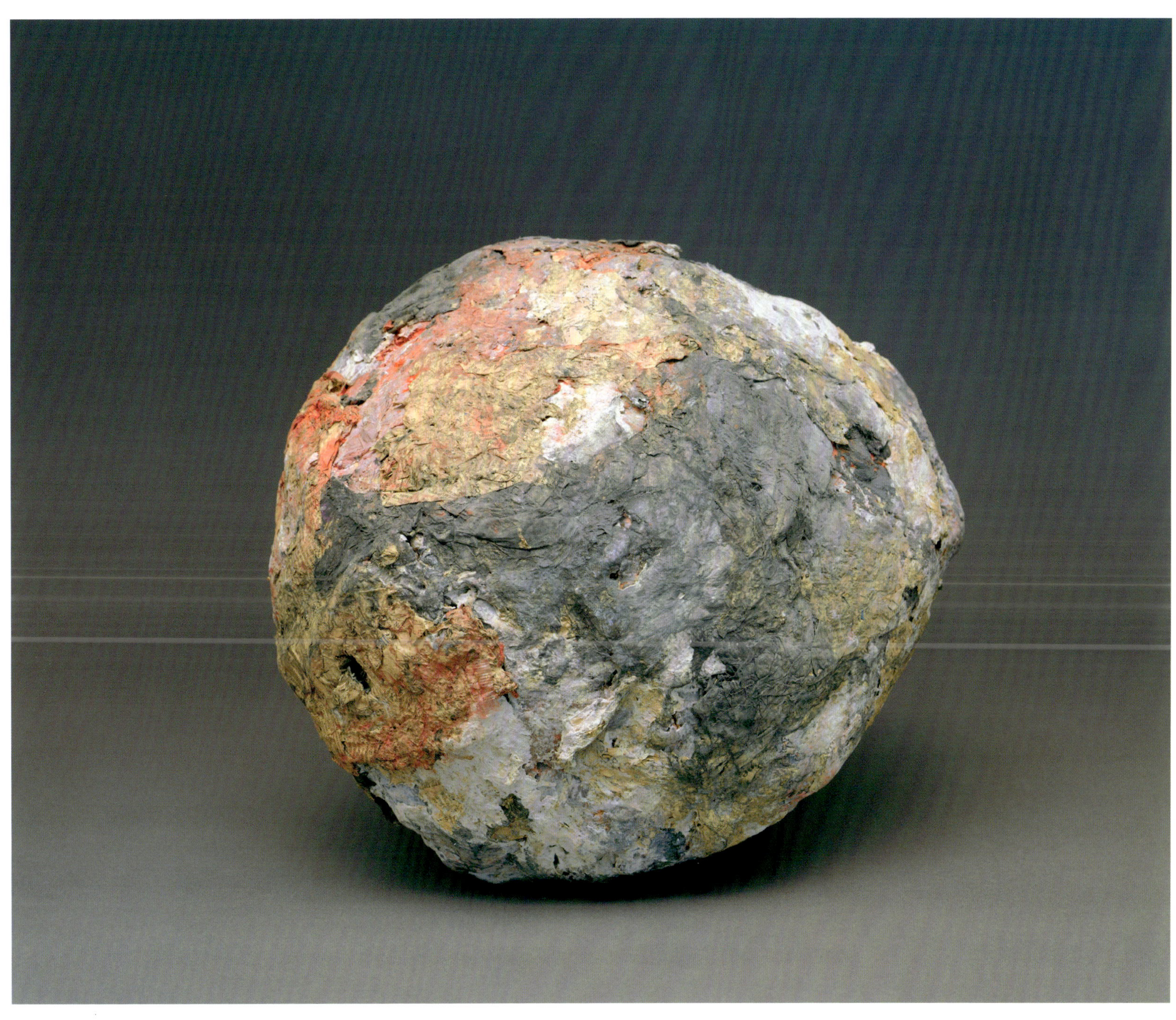

Siah Armajani (American, b. Iran, 1939)
Fibonacci Discovery Bridge (model) 1988
Wood, stain
12 ¾ x 8 ½ x 70 inches

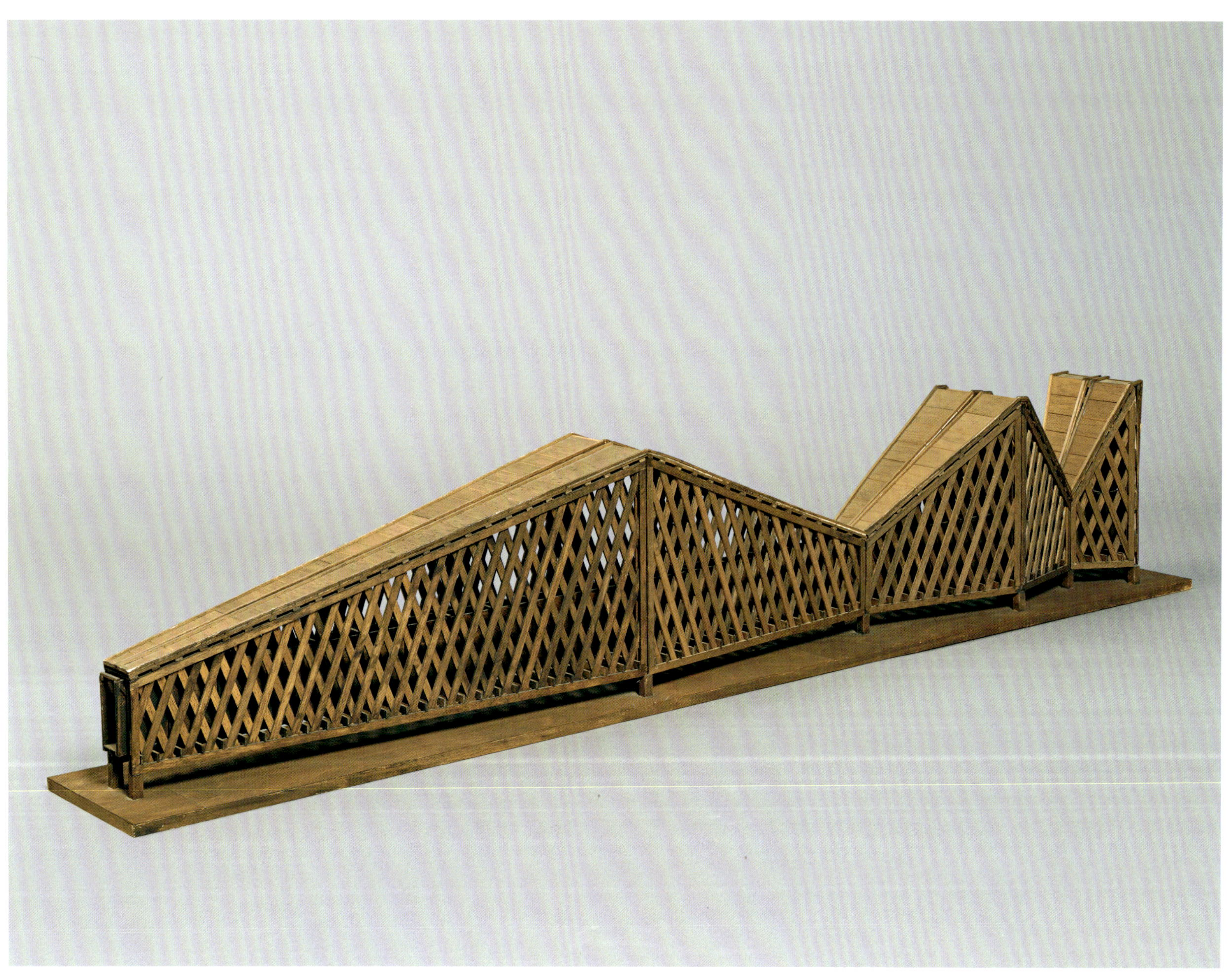

Bernd and Hilla Becher (German, b. 1931 and 1934)
Lime Kilns, Harlingen, Holland 1963
Black-and-white photograph
11 ¾ × 15 ¾ inches

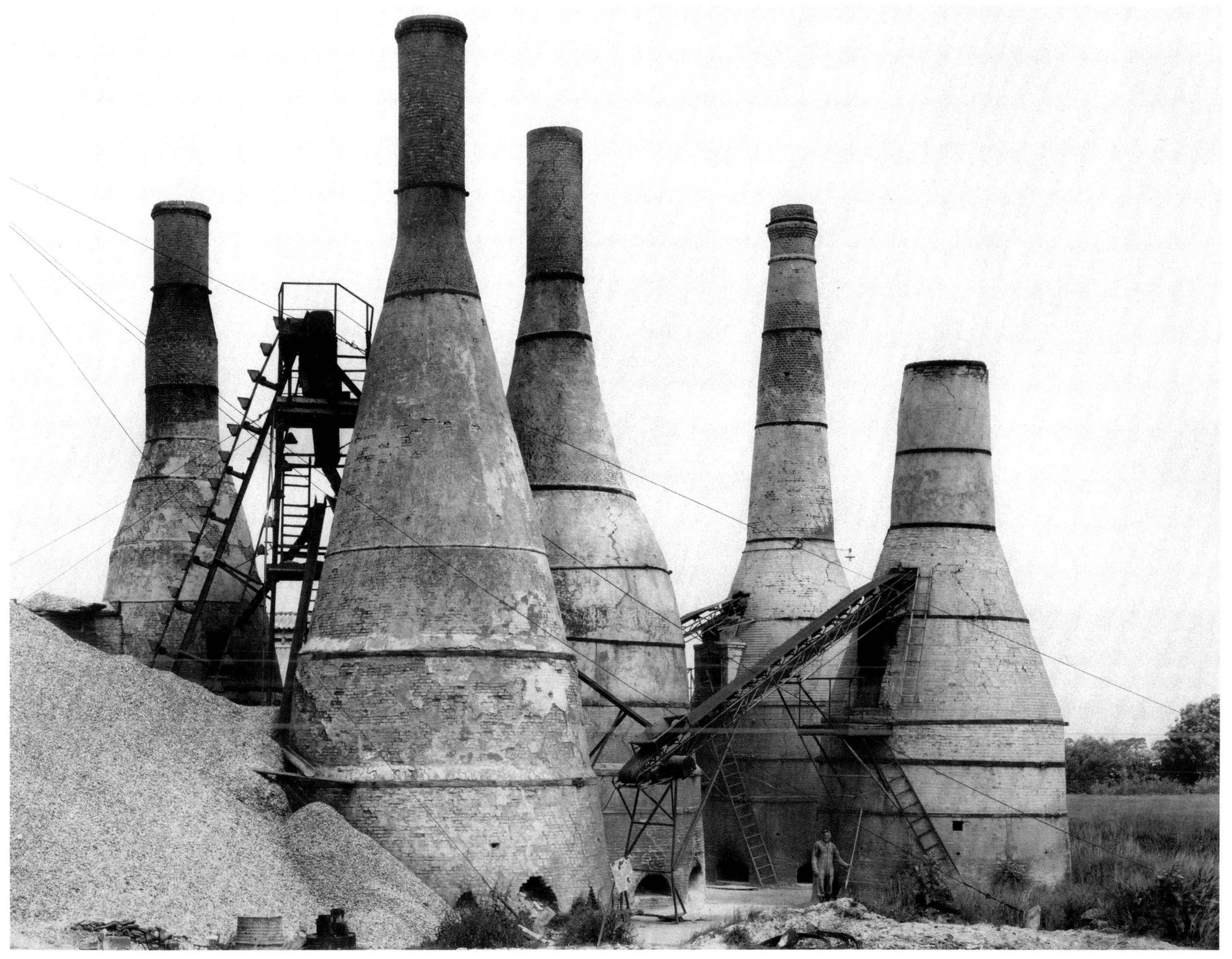

between this determined search for specimens and an anthropological expedition was apparent to the Bechers; they referred to their building records as "typologies." The structures they photographed were often in disuse and disrepair, and the Bechers were concerned with the urgency of photographing them before their destruction. In their words, "Our problem is a fight against time."[5]

The unique contribution of the Dutch artist Jan Dibbets takes the form of an analysis of visual phenomena. His photographs made in the 1960s follow an image through a series of permutations. Using the camera as a tool, he varied the shutter speed or the aperture setting to produce images in series that explore the way we see. Viewing the work in this exhibition, we experience the passage of time as shadow patterns shift in the space of the Konrad Fischer Gallery in Düsseldorf. This gallery was the scene of several historic international group shows in the 1960s and '70s, and through such contacts Sol LeWitt met many of the artists who are represented in the collection, including his friend Jan Dibbets.

Hiroshi Sugimoto has photographed subjects such as dioramas and waxworks figures in series, which entails seeking them out in a various locations. In a series of photographs shot in movie theaters begun in 1978, he made lengthy exposures of the screens as films were being projected on them, which resulted in ghostly white screens. Although they were taken in different locations, the similarities are apparent, which recalls the photographic typologies made years before by the Bechers.

By 1976 the LeWitt Collection was growing quite large, and the artist arranged to have many of the works housed at the Wadsworth Atheneum in Hartford, Connecticut. The Atheneum's curator of contemporary art, Andrea Miller-Keller, drew upon works in the LeWitt Collection for a series of changing exhibitions she organized. In 1982 a gallery was committed to the display of works from the collection. These programs resulted in broader public exposure for the work.

In the late 1990s the LeWitts purchased a warehouse building in Chester and began a process of consolidating the majority of the collection there. Janet Passehl, who had been Andrea Miller-Keller's assistant at the Wadsworth Atheneum, became curator and registrar of the LeWitt Collection. At the Chester facility, she manages a total of approximately 10,000 works by LeWitt and hundreds of other artists who have formed connections with the LeWitts. The LeWitt Collection initially focused on conceptual art, a significant movement that has influenced the thinking of many artists since it appeared in the 1960s. As a result of its subsequent expansion, the collection now embraces a broad range of styles and expressions that is reflected in the diversity of the works in this exhibition. In recent years, new works by old friends have continued to enter the collection—tributes to the durability of these friendships—even as works by artists born after the earliest work shown here (1961) are added.

1. Interview by the author with Sol and Carol LeWitt, Chester, CT, August 2003.
2. Hans Haacke, statement for exhibition at the Howard Wise Gallery, New York, January 13–February 3, 1968, reprinted in Lucy Lippard, *Six Years: The Dematerialization of the Art Object from 1966 to 1972* (1973; reprint, Berkeley and Los Angeles: University of California Press 1997), 37.
3. Jackie Ferrara, in an interview with Ileen Sheppard Gallagher, *Jackie Ferrara Sculpture: A Retrospective* (Sarasota, FL: John and Mable Ringling Museum of Art, 1992) 11–37; quote on 13.
4. Jeff Wall, "'Marks of Indifference': Aspects of Photography in, or as, Conceptual Art" (1995), reprinted in *The Last Picture Show: Artists Using Photography 1960–1982*, ed. Douglas Fogle (Minneapolis: Walker Art Center, 2003), 35.
5. Bernd and Hilla Becher, in an interview with Lynda Morris, *Bernd and Hilla Becher* (London: Arts Council 1973), unpag.

Jan Dibbets (Dutch, b. 1941)
The Shadows at Konrad Fischer Gallery 1969
Black-and-white photographs mounted on board, pencil, ink
19 ½ x 25 ½ inches

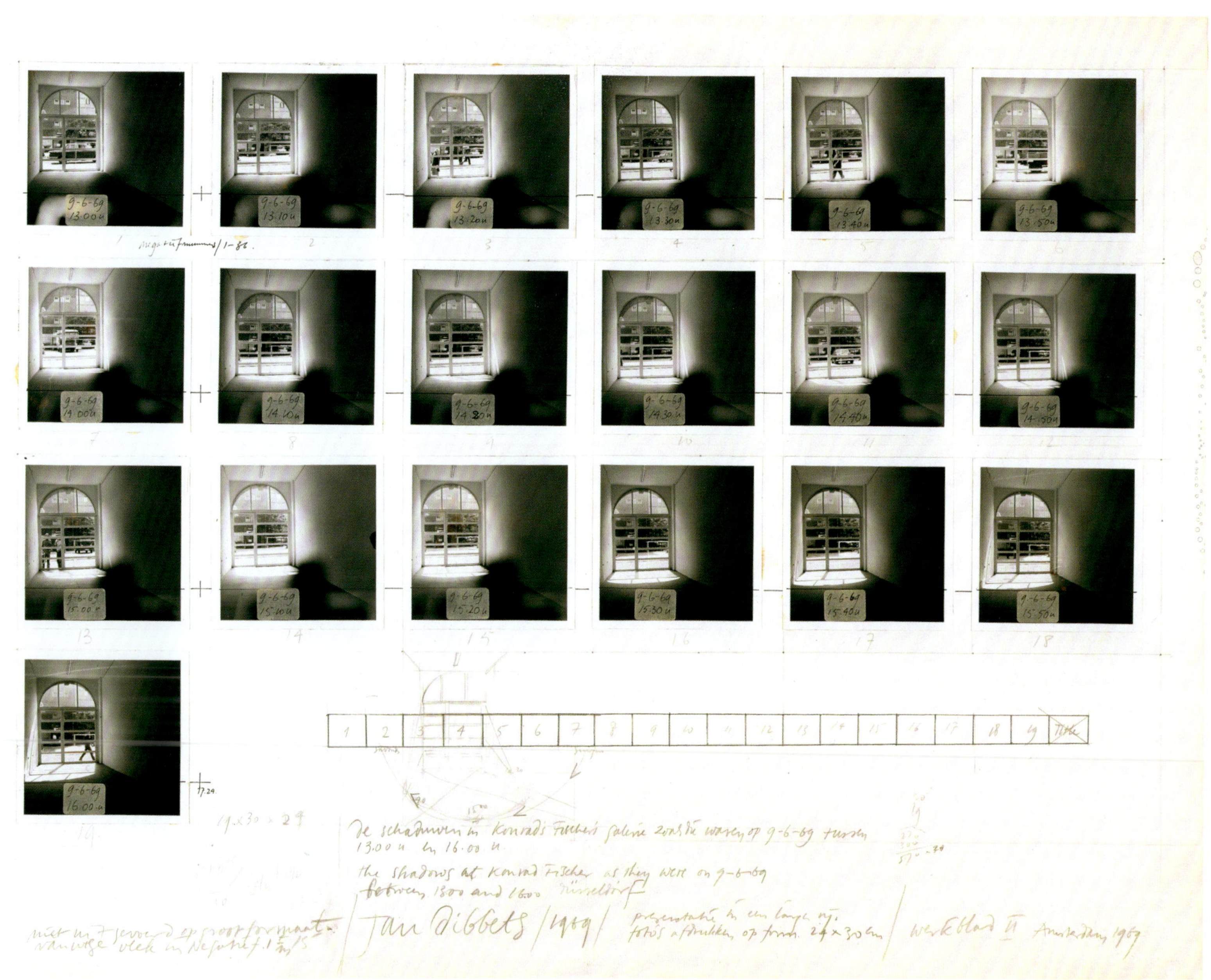

Hiroshi Sugimoto (American, b. Japan, 1948)
Fifth Avenue Theatre, Seattle 1997
Gelatin silver print
19 × 24 inches

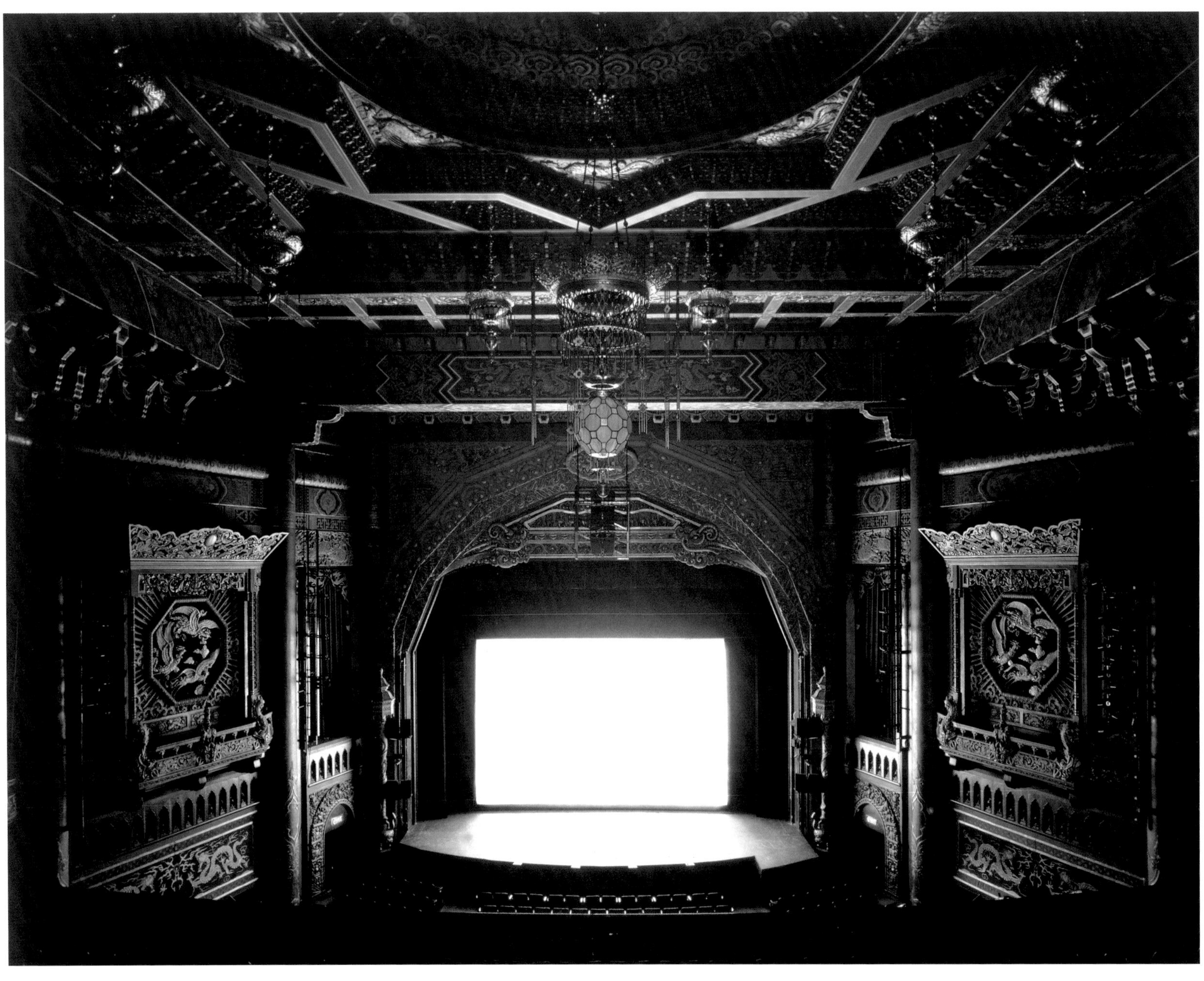

Carl Andre (American, b. 1935) and
Melissa Kretschmer (American, b. 1962)
Cenotaph for Julian Pretto 1996
Sand-limestone blocks, glass, tar, silicone glue
64 × 20 5/8 × 22 5/8 inches

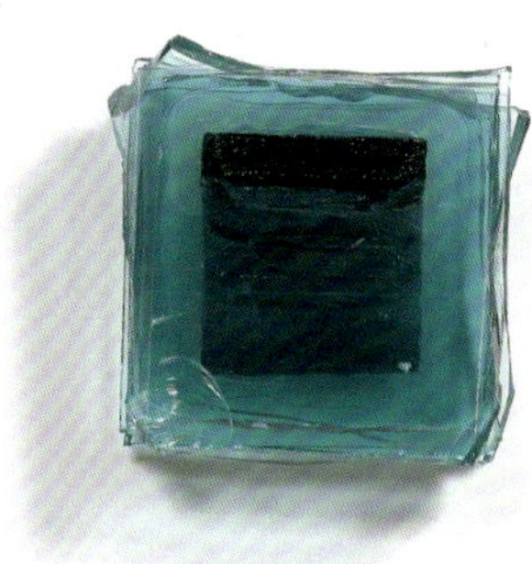

Shirin Neshat (Iranian, b. 1957)
Fervor Series 2000
Gelatin silver print
46 ⅞ × 63 ¾ inches
Published by Barbara Gladstone Gallery, New York, in an edition of 5

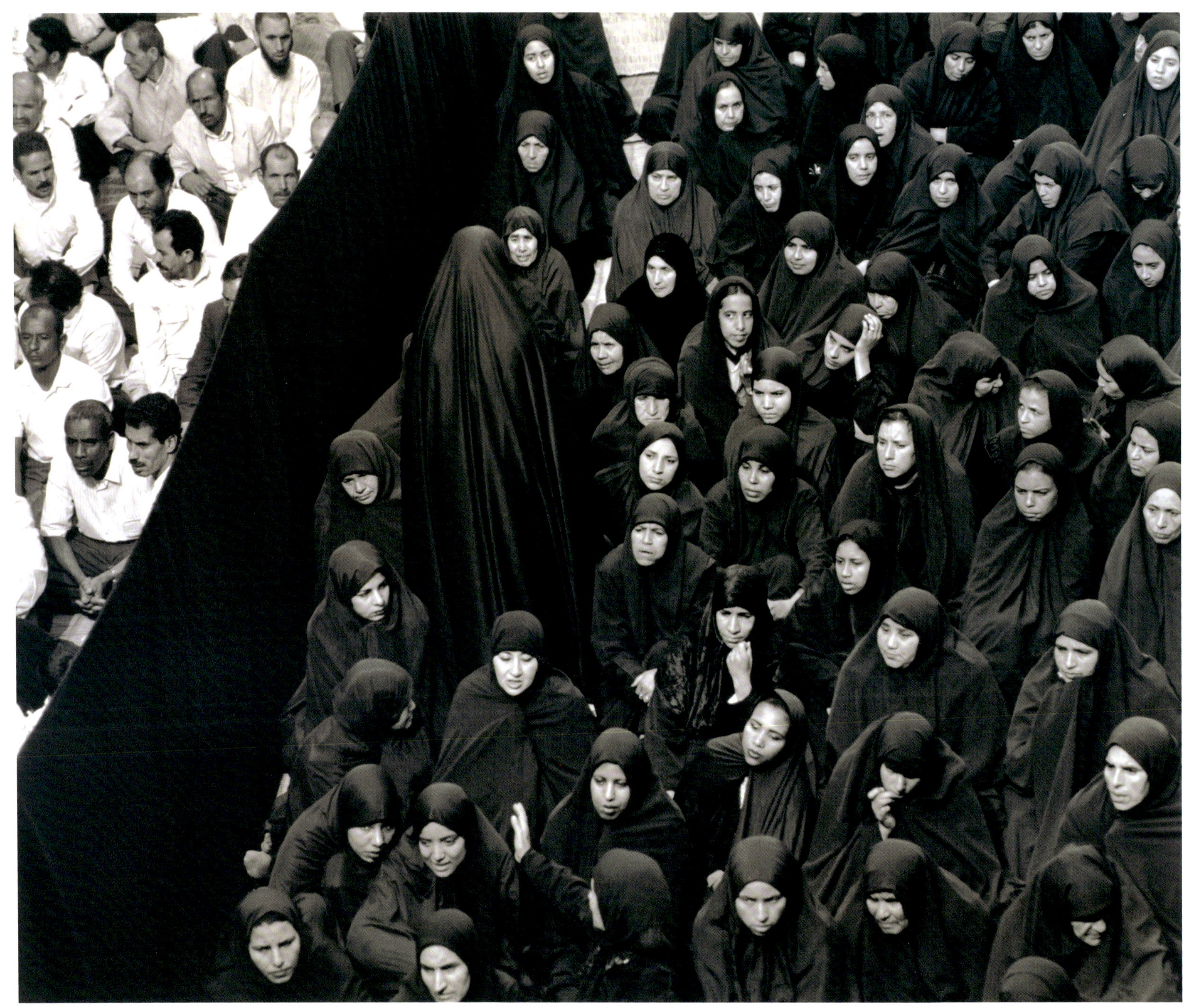

Chuck Close (American, b. 1940)
Self-Portrait 2000
111-color screen print on paper
65 ½ × 54 ⅛ inches
Published by Pace Editions, Inc. in an edition of 80

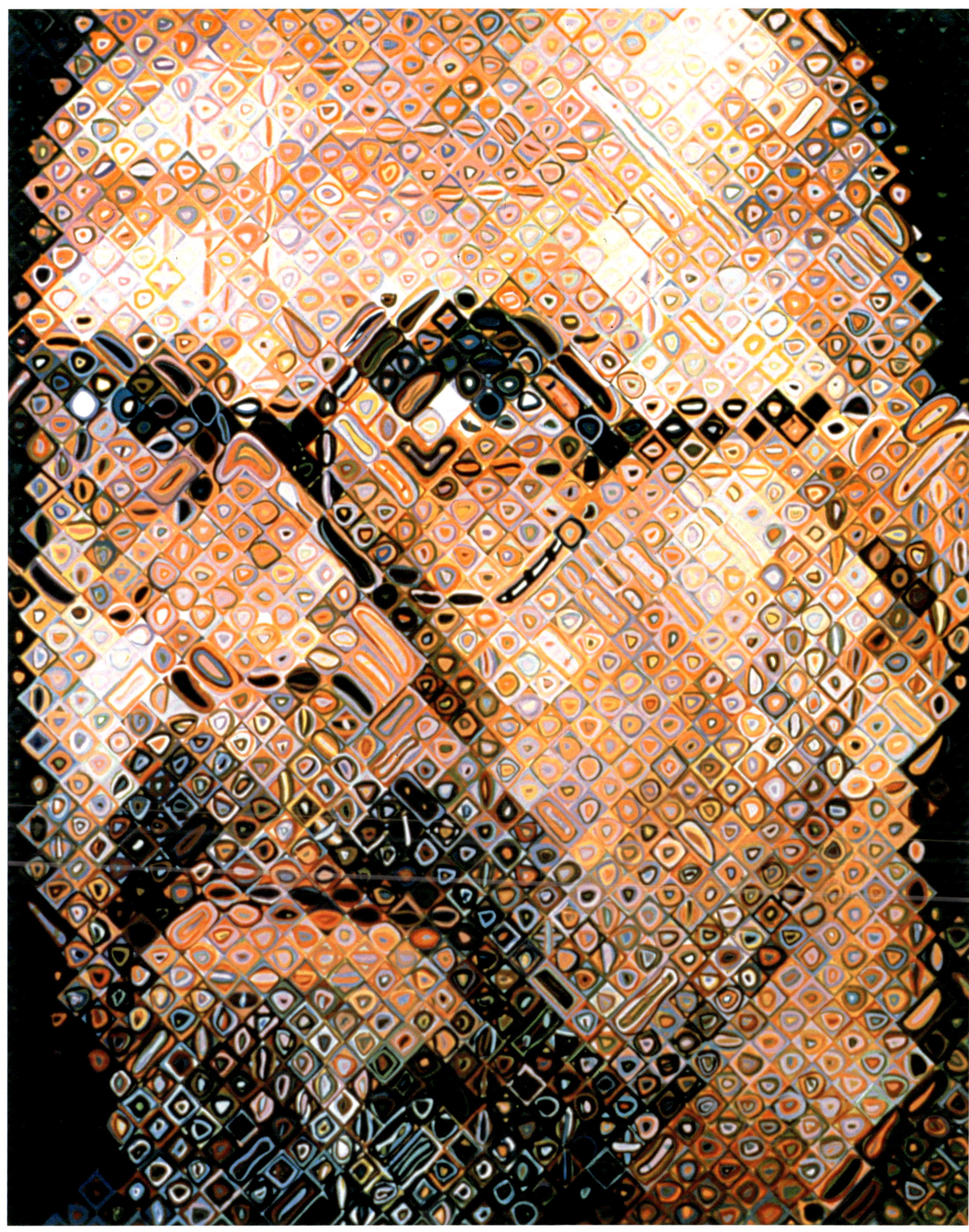

Mel Bochner (American, b. 1940)
D1 (Erased and Turned) 1996
Oil on prepared paper
15 × 20 inches

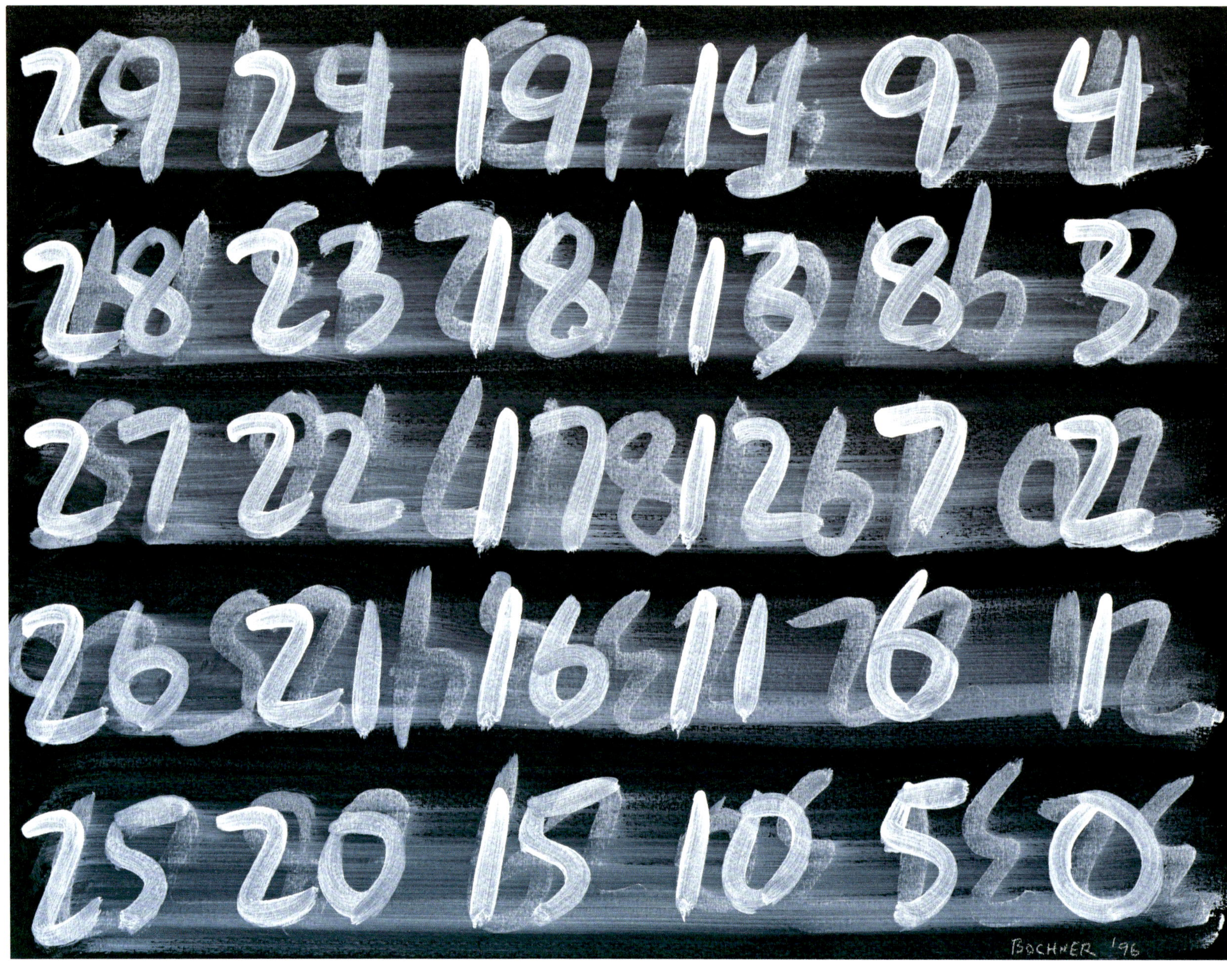

Ian Hamilton Finlay (Scottish, 1925–2006)
Unnatural Pebbles 1981
Cut and polished stone
Freckled Freshet: ½ × 4 × 2 ⅝ inches
Pebbled Brook: 1 ⅛ × 3 ⅛ × 3 ⅝ inches
Stony Stream: 1 ⅛ × 3 × 2 ⅜ inches

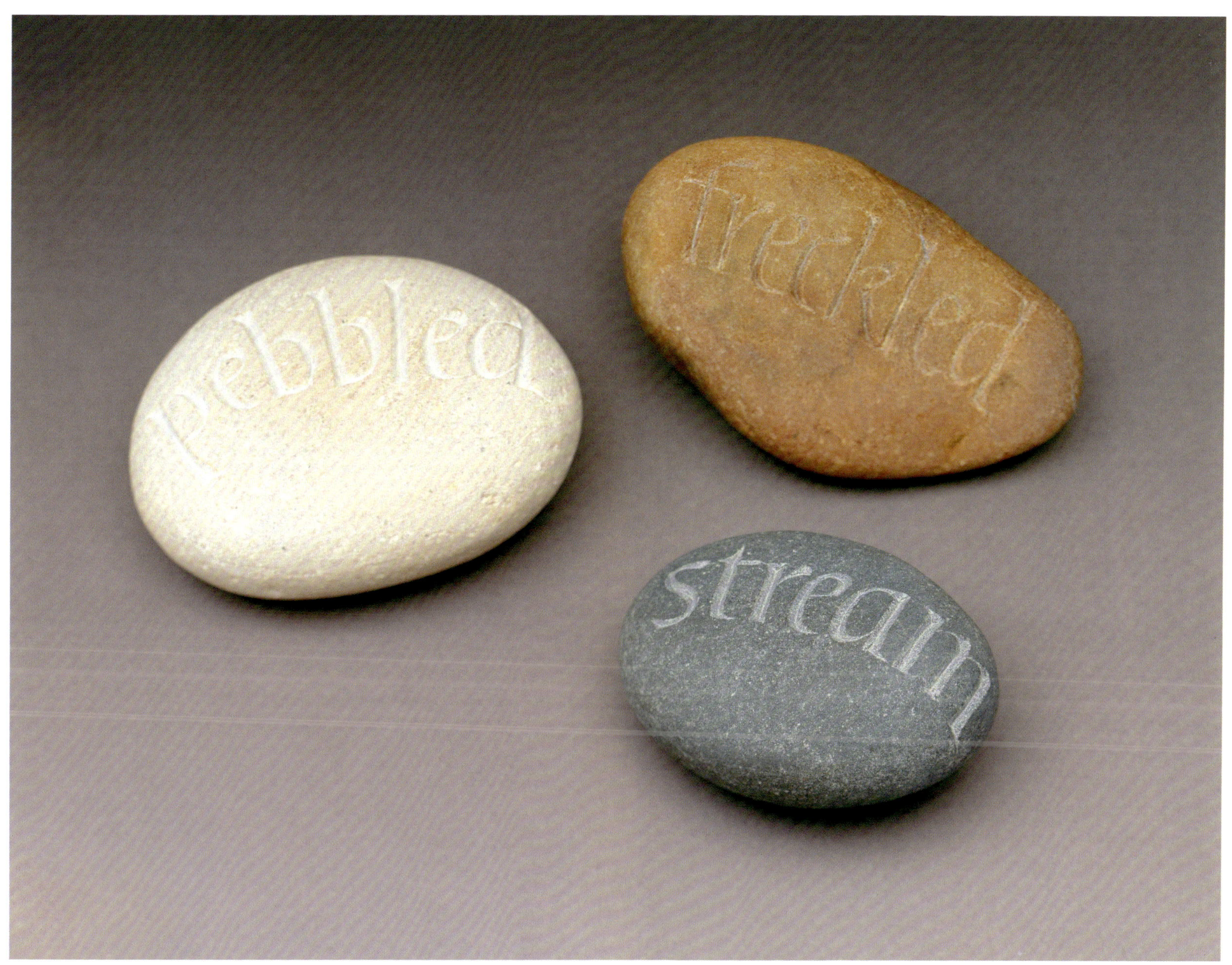

Alex Katz (American, b. 1927)
Allen Ginsberg 1986
Pencil on paper
22 × 15 inches

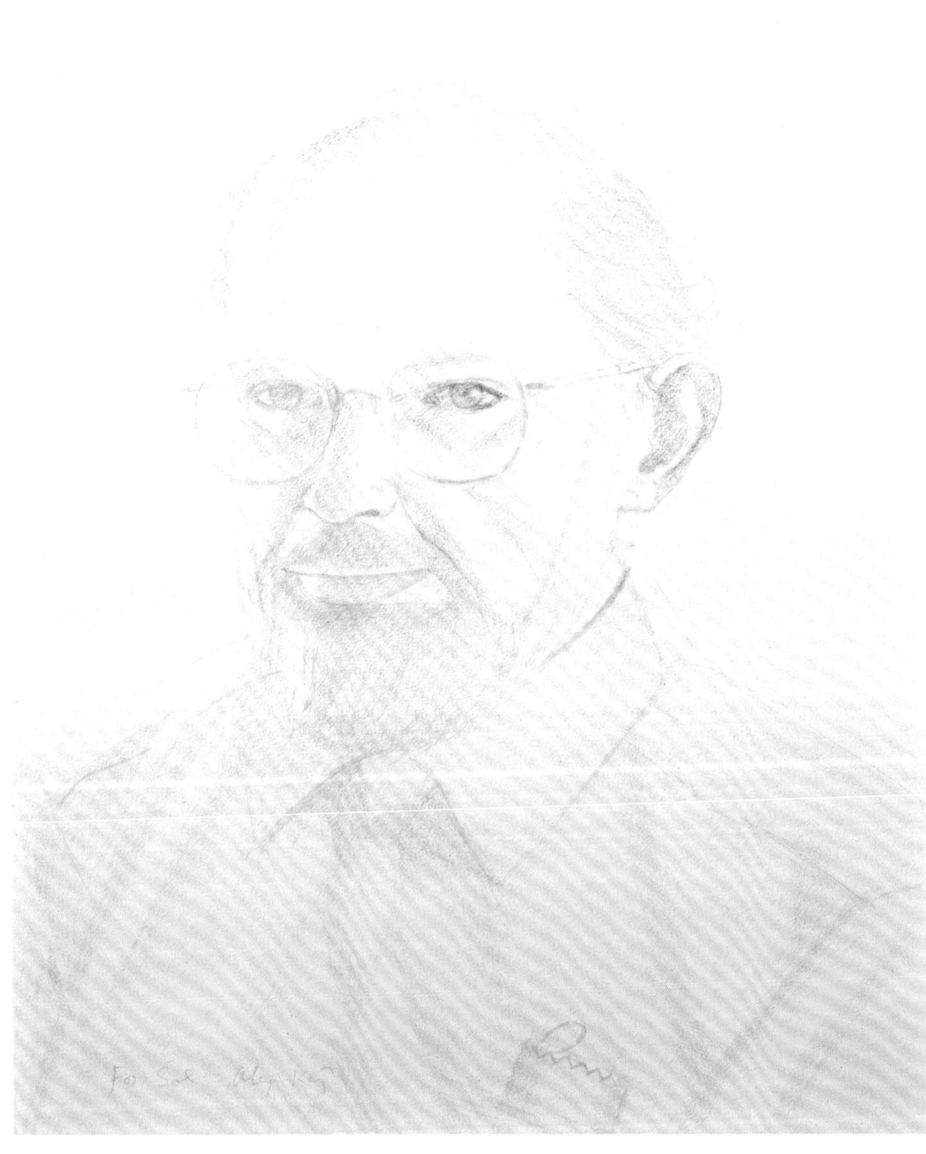

Alice Aycock (American, b. 1946)
From the Story of the Industrial Revolution 1979
Pencil on vellum
14 × 17 inches

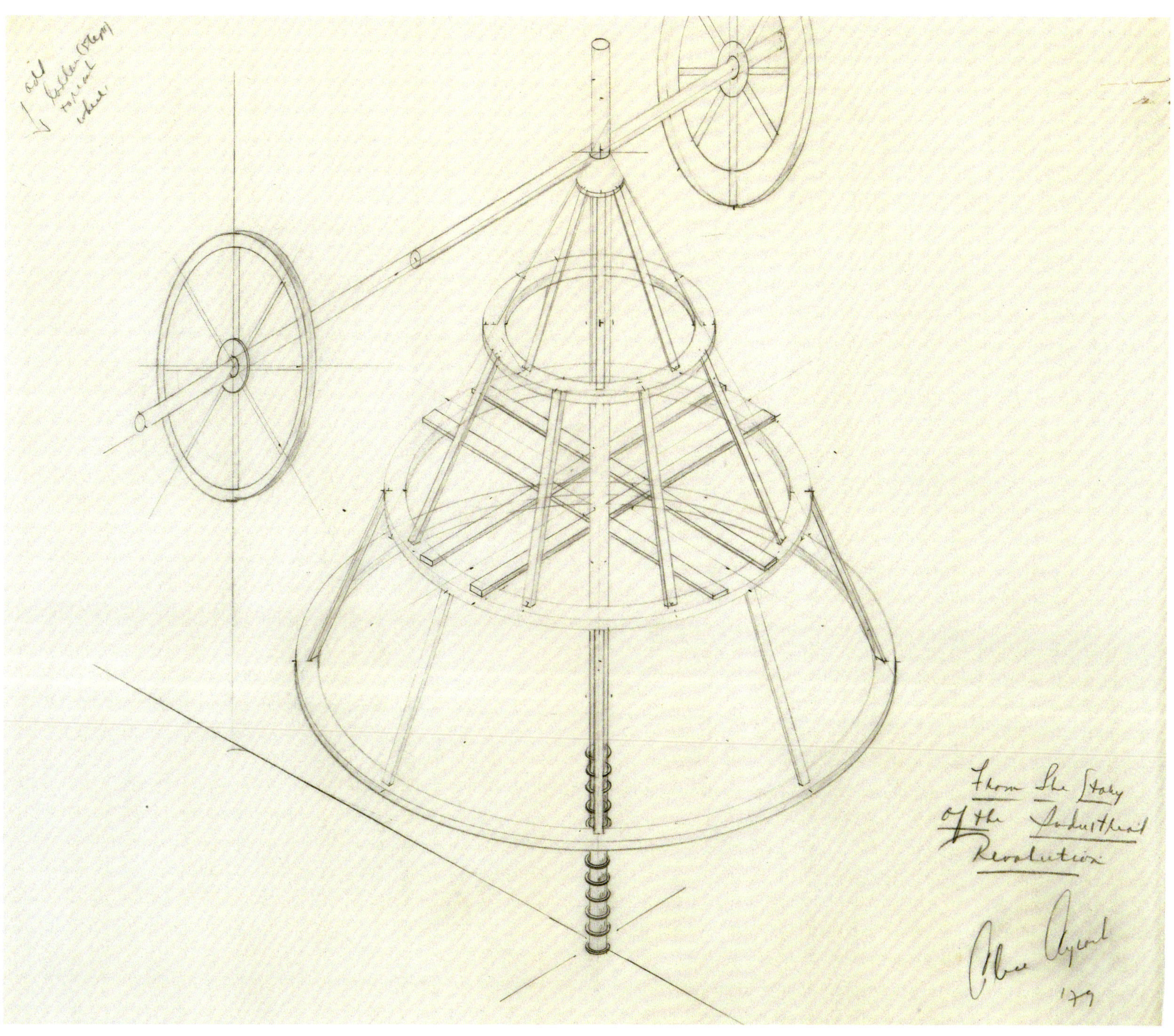

Robert Mangold (American, b. 1937)
Red/Green + Within + (variant) 1983
Acrylic and pencil on wood
24 × 25 ½ inches

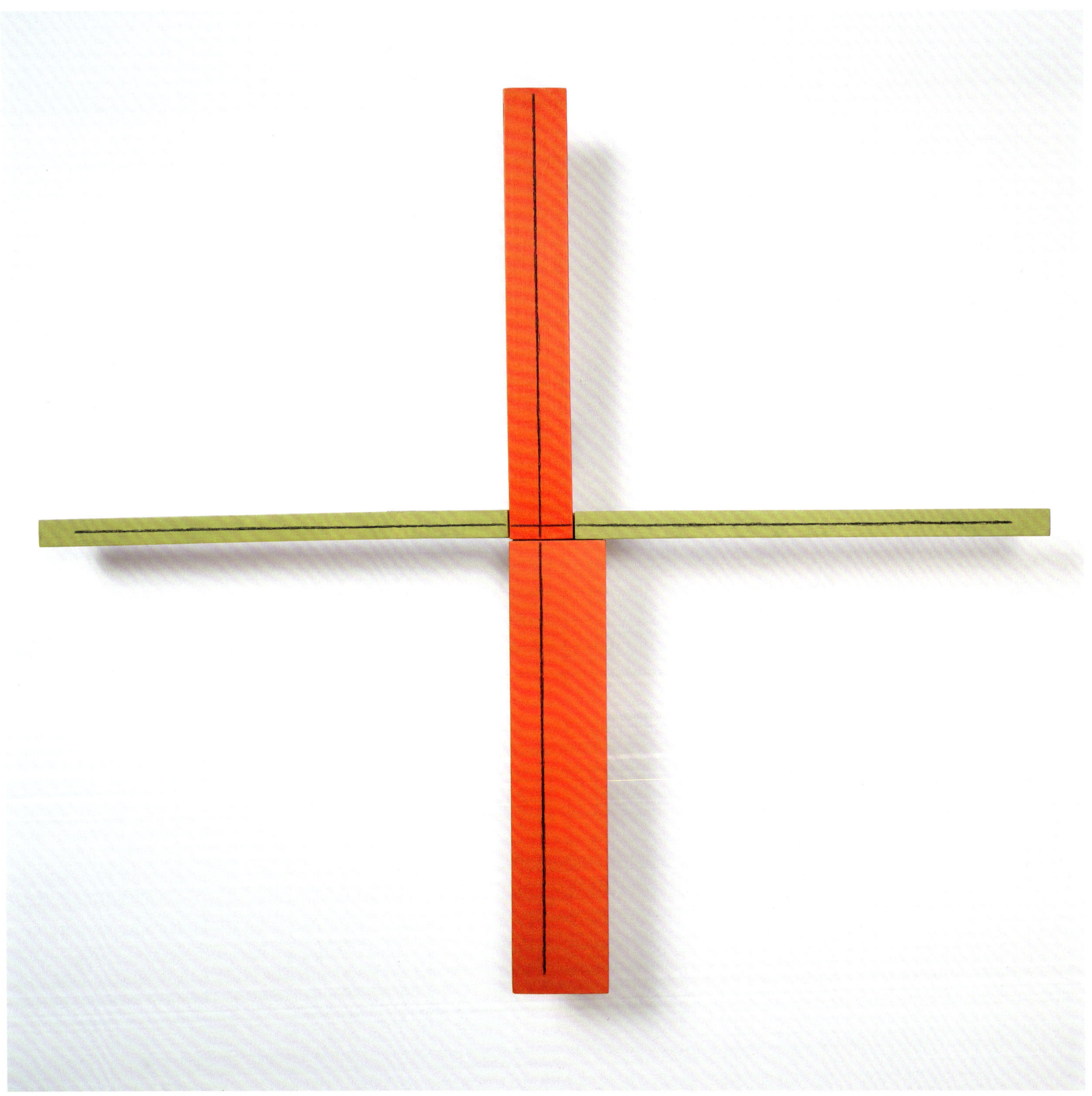

Sylvia Plimack Mangold (American, b. 1938)
Untitled (Study for "Portrayal") 1979
Oil on canvas
24 × 24 inches

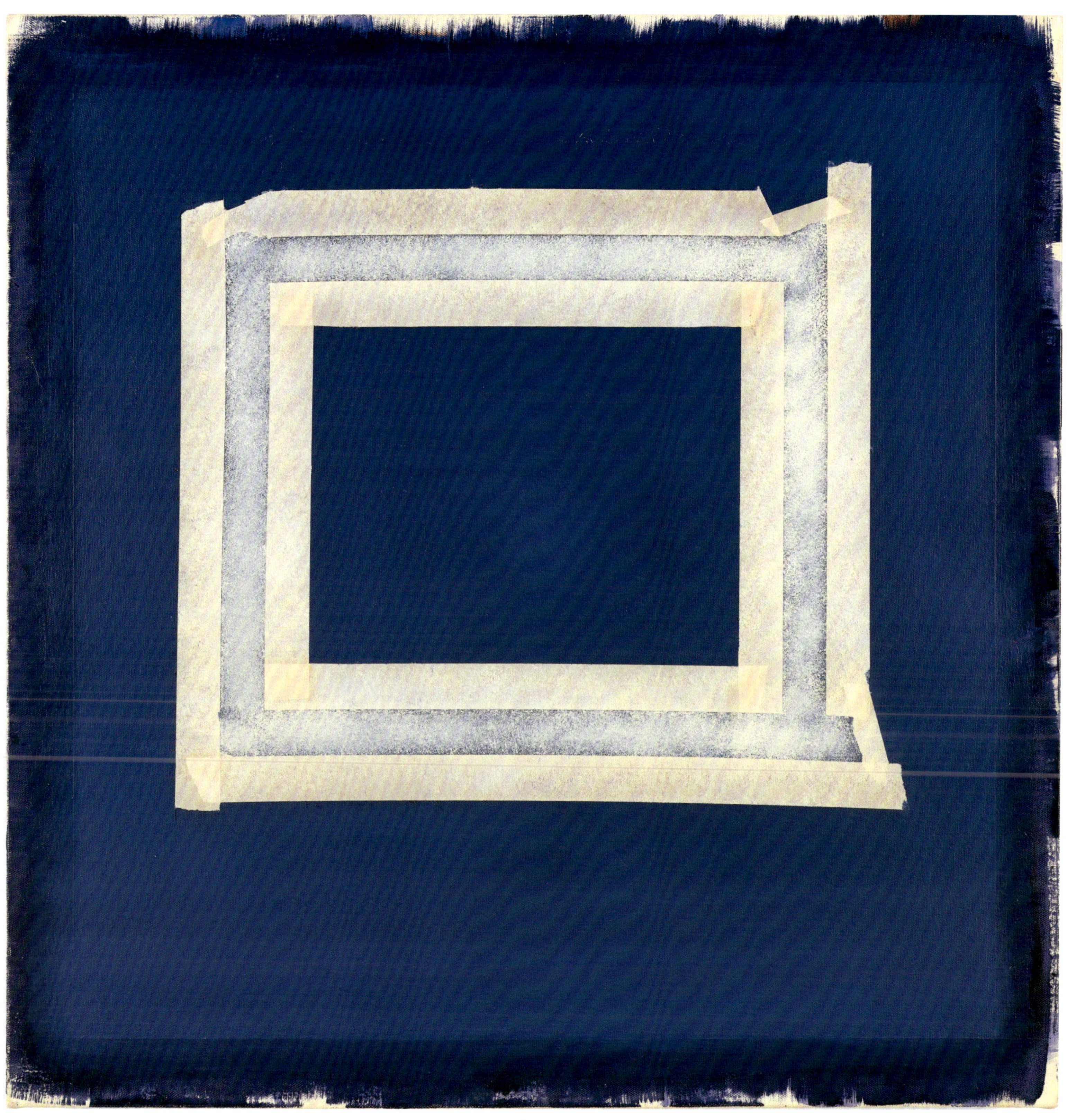

Ree Morton (American, 1936–1977)
Displaced Tree 1972
Watercolor, crayon, graphite on paper
15 × 22 ¼ inches

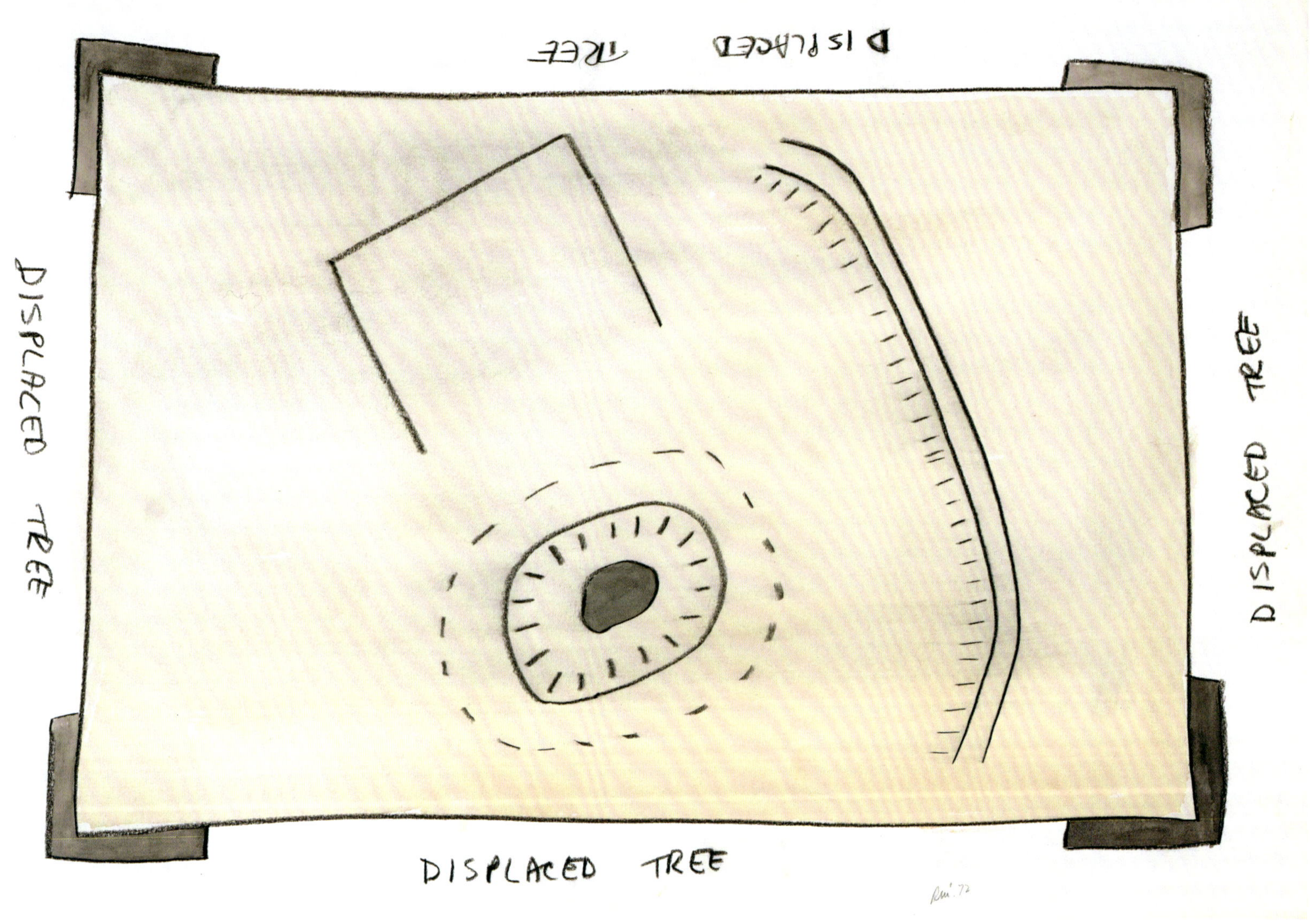

Jonathan Borofsky (American, b. 1942)
I Dreamed Someone Cut up My Duchamp Book 1976
Paint and charcoal on canvasboard
20 × 16 inches

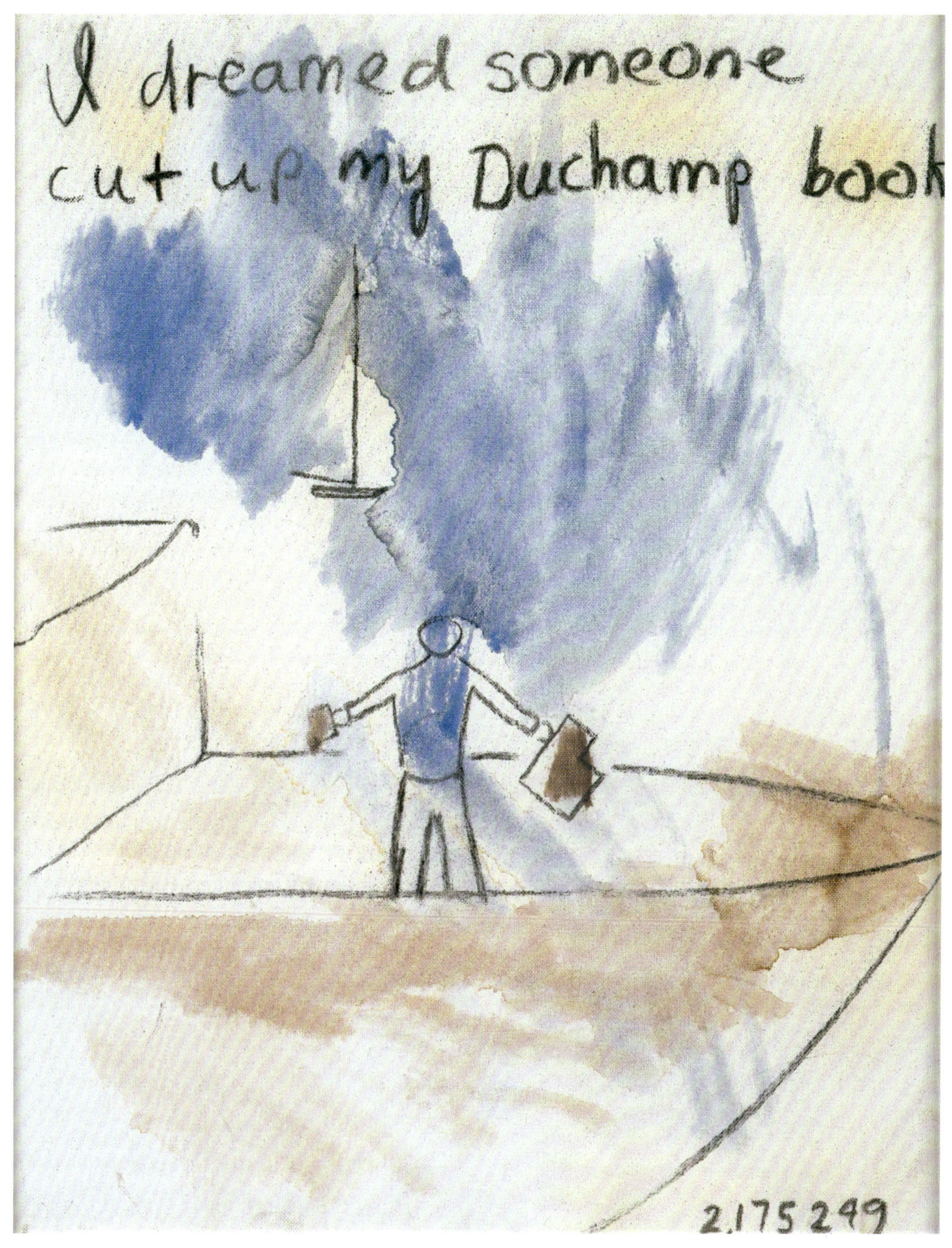

Joel Shapiro (American, b. 1941)
Untitled 1976
Charcoal on paper
38 × 36 ¼ inches

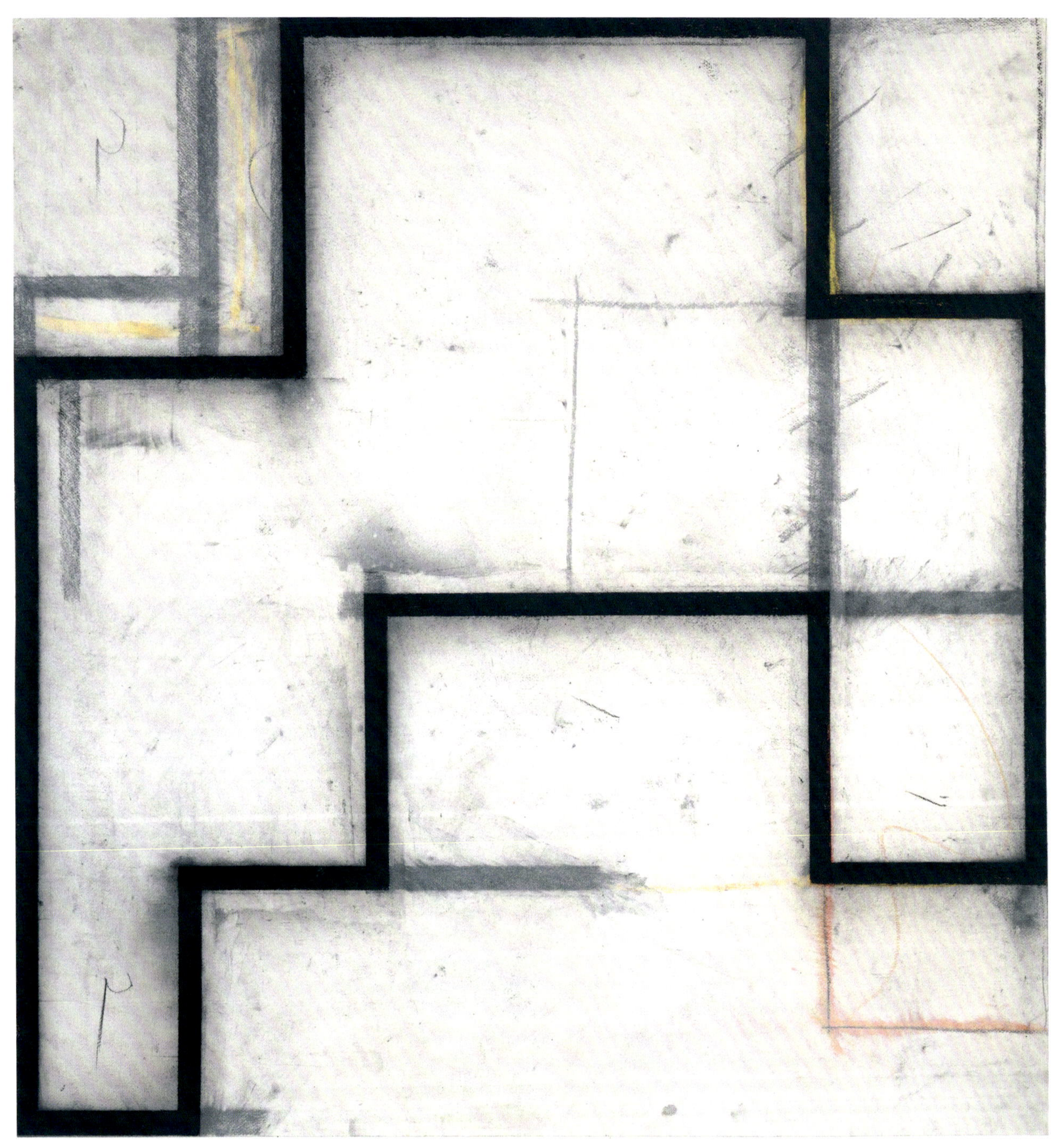

Pat Steir (American, b. 1940)
Black and Blue Sea with Three Spots of Phosphorescence 1997–98
Oil on canvas
72 × 72 inches

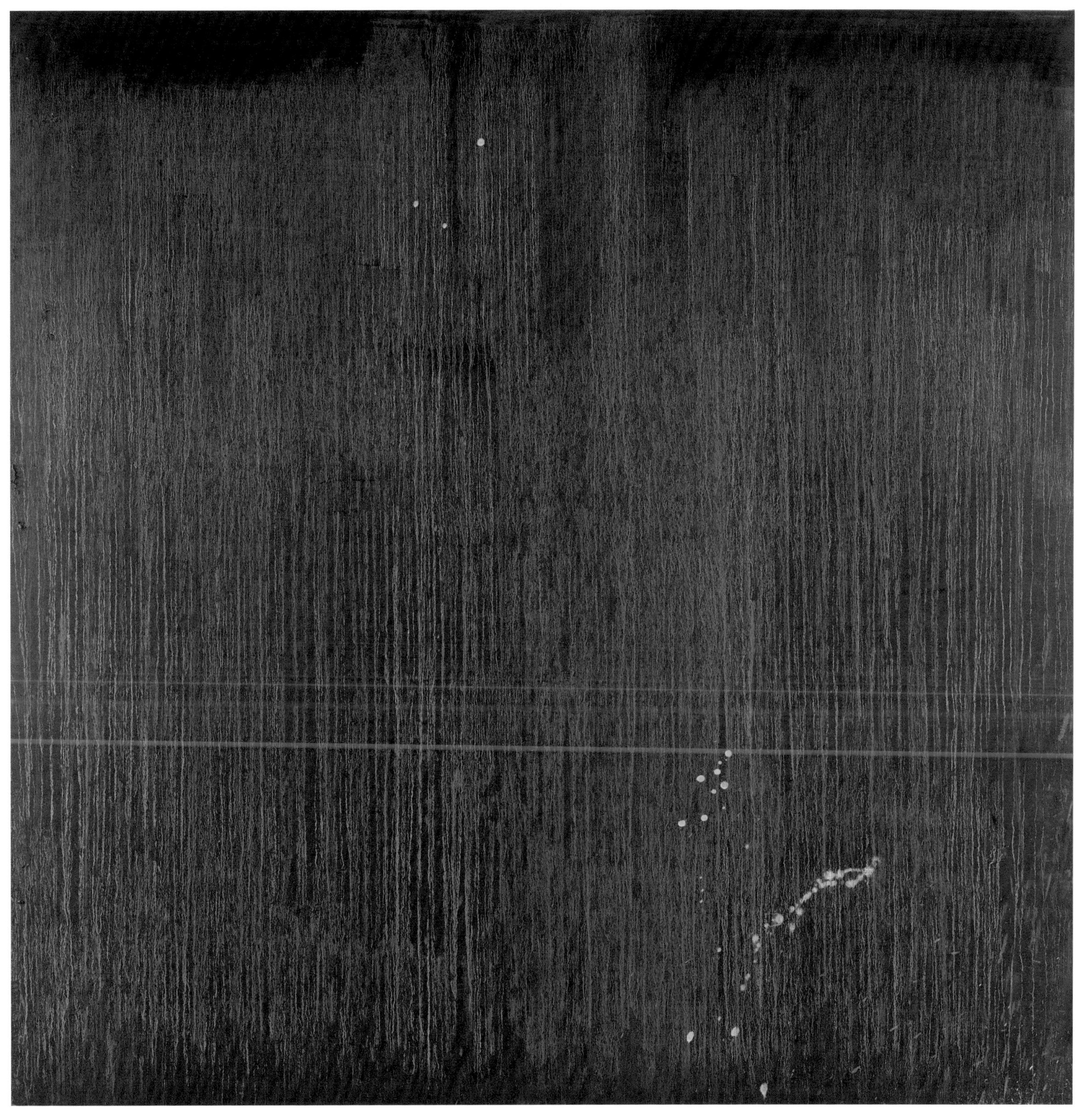

WHO IS SOL LEWITT?

Martin Friedman

On a crisp September evening in 1998, a large bus filled with artists, including Chuck Close, Pat Steir, and Dorothea Rockburne, assorted dealers, collectors, and a scattering of museum world people—my wife Mickey and I among them—slowly wended its way north through crowded Manhattan streets. The festively attired passengers (most in Soho black) were friends of the artist Sol LeWitt on their way to his 70th birthday party at the Wadsworth Atheneum Museum of Art in Hartford, Connecticut. Because commercial vehicles are not permitted on the FDR Drive, buses heading for the Connecticut Turnpike must journey through Harlem, with frequent pauses for stop signs and traffic lights. After crossing the Triborough Bridge, the bus finally made it to the open highway. The birthday party we were heading for had been co-organized by Sol's dear friends and collectors, Janice and Mickey Cartin. The seating arrangements were handled by LeWitt's wife, Carol, and Susanna Singer, LeWitt's business representative since 1980. That so celebratory an event could take place in honor of so publicity shy an artist as Sol LeWitt engendered amused conversation on board. Some marveled that he had permitted the party to take place. As was well known in art-world circles, LeWitt habitually avoided situations where he would be the center of attention and rarely allowed photographs of himself to be included in the catalogues of his exhibitions. "Sol's thinking," says a sympathetic Chuck Close, "is that *no one* needs to know what he looks like. He isn't interested in what he calls 'the cult of the artist.' He wants people to have a relationship with his work, not with him. I respect that attitude and almost wish I had adopted it myself," he adds, a touch wryly. "I would have gotten a lot more work done." Although LeWitt shrinks from public attention, often not even turning up for openings of his own gallery shows, he has long been a loyal regular at the openings of other artists. "When he comes to one of mine," says Close, "I know how much he doesn't want to be there, but he makes the effort to show up. It's very moving when he does, yet it's guilt provoking."

While some of us on the bus had previously traveled to Hartford by car, a trip of about three hours; tonight's journey, it was apparent as the bus navigated through heavy traffic, would take much longer. Shortly after being collected between 6:00 and 6:30 pm at Downtown and Midtown pickup points, the guests were soon pleasantly insulated from the rigors of the journey, thanks to freely poured champagne. The first hour or two of travel was relatively painless, but its length eventually took a toll. Some of the would-be revelers were getting bleary eyed. Awaiting us at the museum, as we staggered off the bus well after 10:00 pm, were more guests, many artists among them.

Despite speculation about whether LeWitt would show up for the party, given his history in such matters, there he was at the entrance to the museum, amiably greeting us, his round face beaming. Sol had been unaware that there would a party in his honor until his daughter Eva inadvertently mentioned it a day or two earlier. By then it was too late to do more than raise objections, so he accepted his fate with grim good grace. That evening, he and Carol had driven from their house in Chester, Connecticut, to the Atheneum, less than an hour away. It was a commute that Sol and Carol had often made for several reasons. Foremost was his long association with the Atheneum, where, as a very young child, he had taken art classes. In the mid-1970s, LeWitt, then living alone in a loft on Hester Street, in New York's Lower East Side, had begun placing his burgeoning collection of works by other artists—paintings, drawings, photographs, and sculptures acquired by trade and purchase—on long-term loan to the Atheneum. This arrangement continued after he married Carol and their moves to Italy and then to Chester. From those holdings, Andrea Miller-Keller, the prescient coordinator of the museum's Matrix exhibitions, would periodically include works from the collection. In these presentations she would explore themes such as location and language, ideas admirably exemplified in works by Sol LeWitt, and in many pieces Carol and he were collecting. In addition to the loan of their collection, the LeWitts had other ties to the museum: in 1994, Carol became a member of its board of trustees, a position she held until 2002. Although successive directors of the Wadsworth

Atheneum may have had varying views about the LeWitt Collection, all seem to have understood its importance to the museum. Best known for its traditional holdings, in particular its Baroque and seventeenth-century Dutch paintings, decorative arts, and nineteenth-century American landscapes, the Atheneum, founded in 1842, also had a noble history of exhibiting and collecting the art of the day. There were many firsts. In 1934, it was the first American museum to present a comprehensive Picasso exhibition and, that same year, to purchase a Miró painting. It was also the first, two years later, to purchase a Mondrian. However, by the 1990s, having the ever-growing LeWitt Collection at the museum was becoming a problem. There was insufficient staff to look after it and not enough storage space to accommodate it. According to Miller-Keller, packages of drawings, paintings, and works in other media would arrive unpredictably from the LeWitts and from galleries throughout the world. Often they were loosely wrapped, with little identification of their contents. Largely because the museum was no longer able to accommodate it, the LeWitts began the collection's withdrawal in the late 1990s, gradually transferring its contents to a warehouse building they had purchased in Chester. There, it would be cared for under the attentive eye of a newly hired curator, Janet Passehl, late of the Atheneum's staff.

Yet another reason the Atheneum held such importance for the LeWitts was that Sol had made several large wall drawings in its building. Some of these were commissioned by the museum, others donated by him. During a brief interval before the birthday dinner, guests could see six LeWitt wall drawings, each in a different building in the museum complex. The earliest, a classic example of LeWitt's use of titles that focus on process, was a 1980 paint and crayon drawing called *White Lines on Color (3 Parts)*. Metaphorically speaking, the length of its subtitle approaches that of the piece. Reading it, however, leaves little doubt about what the artist wanted the work to look like:

> The wall is divided vertically into three equal parts, red, yellow and blue.
> 1st part: On red, white vertical parallel lines, and in the center, a square, within which are white horizontal parallel lines;
> 2nd part: On yellow, white vertical parallel lines, and in the center, a circle within which are white horizontal parallel lines;
> 3rd part: On blue, white vertical parallel lines, and in the center, a triangle within which are white horizontal parallel lines. The vertical lines do not enter the figures.

The cubic forms of the second wall drawing, made in 1989 and executed in color ink washes, occupied the four walls of a small gallery. A 1995 drawing, installed in the museum's front lobby the next year, was composed of "irregular wavy color bands" on two facing walls. The three-story-tall composition of twisting linear shapes was framed within six vertical white-bordered panels. (In 2004, LeWitt would make yet another wall drawing for the Atheneum, *Whirls and Twirls*, formed of segments of bright red, blue, green, and yellow circles, installed above a grand marble staircase, echoing the arch of a doorway below.)

Once the guests were finally assembled, the Atheneum's then director, Peter Sutton, ushered us into the gallery where the dinner would be held. Adorning its walls were selections from the LeWitt Collection. By the time we were seated, the dinner, planned for much earlier that evening, was closer to being a midnight supper. The mood of the guests, especially those who had come by bus, was now revived; the conversation was lively. As dinner concluded, the inevitable encomiums began. The first was a welcoming speech by the silver-haired Sutton, which began with the lofty observation that Hartford was indeed fortunate in that two of its native-son artists—Frederick Church in the nineteenth century, and Sol LeWitt in the twentieth—had brought it great renown. He then noted, with a glance in the direction of Chuck Close and Robert Mangold, that some of LeWitt's fellow artists in the room were there to do him honor. In preparation for writing this piece, I spoke with a number of the party guests about him and his works. When Close and I reminisced about that evening, he laughingly remembered LeWitt's apprehension about what lay ahead. "Sol looked right at me, shook his finger at me, and said, 'Don't you dare!' So of course I didn't." It was about then that LeWitt stood to declare, "No speeches!" Sutton, gamely attempting to stick to the program, turned to the protesting honoree and good-humoredly suggested that at least one such tribute be heard. "No!" was LeWitt's definitive response. The fact that he had been taken by surprise, by a surprise party, doubtless contributed to his annoyance. The room fell silent except for the shuffling of chairs and nervous whispering of the guests. About five minutes later, another would-be speaker, Andrea Miller-Keller, who had been at the museum nineteen years, tried her luck. When she and I reviewed that evening, she remembered Peter Sutton saying, "'Well, Sol, maybe you'll let Andrea come up here, because she's been your friend for so long.' So I got up, reluctantly." No sooner had she begun reading her lighthearted account of LeWitt's artistic journey from New York's Lower East Side to Connecticut's pastoral environs (her talk was titled "From Hester to Chester") than LeWitt once again made his feelings known. Grabbing the papers from Miller-Keller's trembling hand, he stuffed them into his pocket, saying, "I'll read it later."

But more fireworks would illuminate the evening. Rising to his feet, Carl Andre sought to offer his paean to the reluctant birthday boy by sonorously declaring that no other artist had done so much for other artists, or was more generous in spirit than Sol LeWitt. But the subject of this adulation refused to hear it through. After ordering Andre, too, to sit down, he adroitly deflected further compliments by directing our attention to a work by Andre, just across the street from the museum, calling it "the greatest public art installation in America." LeWitt was referring to *Stone Field Sculpture*, a still-controversial 1977 permanent installation of rows of boulders.

Had Andre been allowed to finish speaking that evening, he might well have said something about LeWitt's work in relation to musical structure, a comparison that he and I discussed recently. He likened LeWitt's work to that of Bach, characterizing his large-scale drawings as "compositions orchestrated on the wall."

Among those warily watching the inexorable unfolding of events were a few other artists, thoroughly familiar with LeWitt's work and personality. One was the painter Pat Steir, who instantly grasped what was going on in LeWitt's mind that evening: "Sol doesn't enjoy being in the limelight, but he does enjoy having his work seen," she remarked as we talked about that angst-fraught occasion. Prior to their respective marriages to other partners, she and LeWitt had been close companions through the 1970s and into the next decade. In 1982 LeWitt married Carol Androccio, who was then working at Parasol Press in New York, and Steir wed the Dutch born publisher Joost Elfers. Knowing LeWitt so well, Steir found his fierce resistance to speeches in his honor all too predictable. Asked about qualities she regarded as central to his character, her immediate response was: "generosity and loyalty. You can't do better than that." After a moment of reflection she offered another. "He has a cranky temper. That's true, too."

The aspects of LeWitt's personality that Dorothea Rockburne says she most admires are "his independence of thought and stubborn unwillingness to accept the recognition due an artist of his stature. Sol doesn't belong to any organizations that I know of. When he was put up for membership at the American Academy of Arts and Letters he refused to join. Yet he is very much part of the art machine—you know, the gallery system." One group, however, that she remembers his being part of was an informal association of artists in the 1970s. "They were mostly Minimalists, who would get together to protest various things," she dryly recollects. The group's strongly opinionated attendees included Don Judd, Dan Flavin, Robert Smithson, Robert Morris, Carl Andre, and Richard Serra. "I was the only woman there. The group had an official name, but I have no idea what it was. I nicknamed us the Art Scouts because I thought that was kind of funny. There was a series of meetings, but I don't think much was accomplished. There was a lot of b.s. going down, but Sol was always very careful to stop us from getting into self-aggrandizement and self-promotion, which could easily have happened in about two seconds. He kept the discussions very much on the straight and narrow. That's pretty much been his way."

A few years later, LeWitt, chronically chary of formal arts organizations, would have an active role in founding one. In 1976 he, along with the critic Lucy Lippard and others, established Printed Matter, whose objective was to distribute artists' books.

Shortly after Barry Le Va became a permanent resident of New York in 1970, he was invited by Smithson and Serra to attend those artists' meetings. Before that move, the then twenty-nine-year-old sculptor had been teaching at the Minneapolis College of Art and Design. As the youngest attendee, Le Va recalls, he was more an observer than a participant. One topic of concern to many of the artists in those politically charged times, he remembers, was whether or not to participate in international exhibitions, such as the upcoming 1972 Documenta, and if so, under what conditions. Since many of the artists were involved with works that would be site specific, there was concern about who would install them, if funds were not provided by the exhibition's organizers.

The central issue was that of the artists' control over how and where their work could be shown. Although Le Va now remembers those meetings as "pseudo-political," he acknowledges that they provided invaluable opportunity for him to meet fellow artists, especially Sol LeWitt. As does Rockburne, he remembers LeWitt as a calm, rational presence during those often heated sessions. In 1967, when Le Va had been a student at Otis Art Institute in Los Angeles, he encountered his first exhibition of LeWitt sculptures at the Dwan Gallery in Los Angeles's Westwood district. "It knocked me out," he told me. "It was an exhibition that showed nine stages of open cubes. They started on the floor and progressed upward to about seven feet." What he had encountered was *Serial Project #1 (Set A)*, the first part of a 1966 four-part white-enamel-painted aluminum work. "It was not about linear thought," Le Va remembers vividly. "I saw a language—and so many possibilities, so many options within a single piece. It was as though these variations could continue infinitely and not be confined to the gallery. It was incredibly moving."

The evening at Hartford lurched to its conclusion. Sol had definitively made his point: no speeches. Who would dare? Guests rose from their tables, some wandered aimlessly around the galleries, and soon all were heading for the exit. A few of the more foolhardy ones, I among them, paused to offer happy birthday wishes to LeWitt. As we shook hands, I cheerily said, "Welcome to my side of the decade!" observing that I had turned 70 just a few years earlier. "Well," he responded, his steely eyes focused on me and still in combat mode, "it doesn't seem to have done much for you." As the exodus continued, those who had come by bus resignedly climbed aboard the waiting vehicle for the long haul back.

▣

So who is Sol LeWitt? He is certainly known for a great deal more than his rejection of praise for his artistic accomplishments, and his generosity to other artists (which is better known). The esteem his work is held in by younger, as well as established artists is decidedly warranted. However, before attempting to characterize that work, a brief history of my friendship and association with him.

LeWitt was a periodic visitor to the Walker Art Center, where I was the director, in the 1970s and '80s, during which time we got to know each other. My wife and I sometimes saw Sol and Carol in Spoleto during our trips to Italy; though they travel there less these days, the LeWitts have a house in this Umbrian town north of Rome. LeWitt was initially represented in the Walker Art Center's collection by two important three-dimensional works. In 1974 the museum purchased the 1966 *Cubic Modular Piece No. 2 (L-Shaped Modular Piece)*, a white-painted metal cagelike structure that suggested a side and partial side of a towering rectangular form. In 1987, another monumental white-painted work was added. Made in 1984 and titled *Three x Four x Three*, it consists of nine giant open cubes stacked three cubes high, like an off-center pyramid. Since then, the museum has added other LeWitt pieces, notably a 1996 concrete block structure installed in the adjacent Minneapolis Sculpture Garden.

In 1984 the Walker acquired a wall drawing by LeWitt. It is actually a series of drawings that read as a single continuous work. He made it for a low-ceilinged, twenty-five-foot-square space just a few steps down from the museum's lobby. I had invited him to Minneapolis early that year to look over this site, hoping he would come up with an idea for unifying this awkward space whose walls were pierced by an inordinate number of doors and openings, which provided access to a new gallery, a print room, a library, and the Education Department. Some of them opened to an elevator, the basement, and the public restrooms. Would LeWitt even consider making a wall drawing for it? I asked him, hesitantly. Yes, he would, was his calm, reassuring answer. So began a long-distance design project that utilized a cardboard mockup of the nettlesome space made for him by the museum's exhibition crew. He would work on ideas for the wall in Italy that summer, he said. A few months after his visit, a small parcel containing the cardboard model arrived. Its previously blank walls were now adorned with huge circles, squares, trapezoids, and parallelograms in tones of blue, ocher, and a deep red verging on terra cotta. What a perfect concept for that impossible space, I thought, and immediately phoned Sol in Spoleto to tell him how pleased I was. The project was now on track. A month or so later, Jo Watanabe, one of LeWitt's New York assistants, arrived in Minneapolis to execute the drawing. Watanabe has worked on LeWitt's projects since the mid-1970s. (Though Jo and his wife, Sachi, were invited to the 1998 party at Hartford, they never made it to the bus.) With assistance from the museum exhibition crew, he rolled several coats of white latex paint onto the four walls of the room, After carefully laying out LeWitt's scheme in pencil on the now slightly textured walls, he and the crew carefully outlined its shapes with strips of masking tape. The medium for the drawings was to be a special variety of India ink produced in spectrum colors made by the German ink company Pelikan. As with his other wall drawings in this medium, LeWitt specified that the colored ink be used not full strength but diluted with water and applied to the masked-off areas of the wall in successive transparent washes by means of cloth dipped in the solution. It was a process roughly akin to glazing over white areas in oil paint. As one wash was applied over another, the color of the shape being worked grew ever more luminous. During the few days it took to make *Four Geometric Figures in a Room*, visitors to the museum would pause, enthralled, as they watched it take form.

Though Watanabe had access to the painted cardboard model of the room, he brought with him a rough sketch of LeWitt's to work from. He told me that LeWitt's directions for wall drawings could vary from basic to quite detailed. “Sometimes Sol just gives us a description of the work,” he said, not long ago, as we talked about his work on the 1984 Walker Art Center piece. A decade or so later, LeWitt turned to another medium, acrylic paint, for these expansive works. As Watanabe explained, like the Pelikan inks, acrylic could be diluted and used as washes; it could also be applied opaquely as high-intensity color, a means of application typical of many of the artist’s recent wall works.

One of the most intriguing aspects of LeWitt’s imagery over some forty-five years has been its varied and at times almost playful relationship to geometry. His shapes have ranged from the austere and formalistic cubes of the early 1960s to the increasingly lyrical, even insouciant, curves that characterize his wall drawings and structures. Though LeWitt was initially grouped with the Minimalists in the 1960s because of his penchant for spare geometric figures, in spirit he was never part of that camp. However much his three-dimensional structures of that period may have suggested a connection, they differed markedly from the highly reductive unitary shapes favored by Donald Judd, Robert Morris, Carl Andre, and other Minimalist stalwarts. LeWitt arrived at his distinctive iconography early in his career through systems of his own invention. In that important respect, he was a conceptualist, well before that term found general use in art world circles. In fact, he has been frequently characterized as “the father of conceptual art,” primarily because of his seminal writings, “Paragraphs on Conceptual Art” (1967) and “Sentences on Conceptual Art” (1969). In the process of art-making, numerical systems, serial systems, and instructional ones based on language provided a kind of insulation from what he and his Minimalist brethren regarded as the perils of expressionism—by which they meant the aftereffects of Abstract Expressionism. Not that these young artists were even remotely dismissive of the achievements of that heroic generation, LeWitt made clear to me during an interview in 1999. Rather, he continued, it was that the movement had run its course before the end of the 1950s and its legendary figures had repeated themselves. “Pollock was painting Pollocks, well after his greatest period. And Kline was getting into color,” he added, a touch sadly.

Unlike his Minimalist compeers, LeWitt was never especially interested in distilling a form to its hard-edged essence. Instead, his interest has consistently been in what happens to it under radically changing conditions of scale, materials, and repetition. His signature cube, for all its apparent stasis, is actually a dynamic unit—a leading character in his ever-changing scenarios. It takes on various personalities as it undergoes constant metamorphoses in size, surface, materials, and complexity. The process has gone something like this: Take a cube—any cube—and see what happens when one or more of its sides is removed. Or, for that matter, if *all* sides are removed and only its outline remains. Or, what happens if most of the cube disappears and only a corner is left? What if the cube is repeated in different sizes or sliced into at various angles to generate blocky new shapes? Such questioning is reflected in shapes LeWitt has employed in drawings on paper and the wall, and in his three-dimensional works.

LeWitt has always moved fluidly back and forth between two and three dimensions. Ideas about scale, repetition, and progression embodied in his wall drawings have their equivalents in his three-dimensional pieces, which he obdurately refers to as structures—not sculptures. For all their formal purity, LeWitt’s structures are never sterile exercises in geometry. Whether his “open cubes” of the 1960s and ’70s, the multifaceted iceberg shapes of the “complex forms” of the late 1980s and early ’90s, or the concrete block pieces that followed—there is a humanist quality about them. The open cubes, for example are speculations about the relationship between solid and void. Some of those structures, composed of an infinity of thin-edged small cubes, lose their dimensionality and dissolve into atmosphere. Aside from elegance of proportion, their most arresting quality is spatial ambiguity. In works such as these, LeWitt’s art verges on the metaphysical.

For all of his commitment to impersonal processes, his work is strongly personal in feeling. As Chuck Close acutely remarked about LeWitt’s system-derived approach, “So much conceptual work looks as though it had been phoned in, but not Sol’s. Because his systems are so open-ended they just keep spawning more and more ideas.”

Although Conceptualism led many an artist to dry results, LeWitt has used systems to lively effect. The most basic of them was the grid, from whose squares his geometry arose. It was the template for his drawings and three-dimensional pieces. During the last decade he has used it to generate a series of three-dimensional works that might be described as “anti-cubes.” With the help of a computer-savvy technician, these configurations have originated in virtual space. Rising from intersections of a grid drawn as though flat on the floor are verticals of different heights. Through the magic of the computer, these verticals are connected with dipping lines. The undulating shapes in these drawings, when rendered three-dimensionally in shiny black or intensely colored fiberglass, suggest the topography of some exotic alien world. A far cry from the cubes he has long been identified with, they are products of logic as capricious as it is analytical. A few of these then seemingly uncharacteristic objects were last-minute inclusions in LeWitt's 2000 San Francisco retrospective, where, predictably, they surprised even those of his devotees familiar with every stylistic shift his work has gone through.

These yet-to-be-classified aberrant objects are, in fact, closely related to the wall drawings he had been making lately in acrylic—some of them incorporating languorous curved forms. Unlikely as it may seem on first consideration, a similarly lyrical quality characterizes LeWitt's latest concrete block structures. This was certainly evident in a 2005 installation of two large concrete block pieces in New York's Madison Square Park. There, he used this prosaic gray building material to construct an elegant upside-down pergola and a flawlessly proportioned fourteen-foot-high, eighty-five-foot-long, crenellated serpentine wall.

When I talked about LeWitt's use of systems with a few other artists, for the most part their views were like Close's. "So much conceptual art can be clinical in feeling but Sol's isn't," Robert Mangold told me. "It has wit and humor that always makes it surprising. The way his mind runs from one idea to another is just amazing." Sometimes, he says of LeWitt's system-derived imagery, "I wonder if Sol has any idea what his things will end up looking like before he makes them." When I asked Pat Steir if she thought that systems were LeWitt's way of finessing the artist ego issue, she was dubious. "I don't think Sol ever thought of it like that. It was his way to get past the idea of expressionism, which I think he equated with a kind of Freudianism. I think that he thought of his work as a return to classical values." Warming to the subject, she added, "In fact, I see his work as a kind of romantic classicism. That may sound like a contradiction in terms, but anyway, that's how I see it." In her view, I wondered, has he made less use of systems in his later work? "Absolutely!" she replied, offering an example: LeWitt's "splat" drawings, her pungent term for the ragged-edged gouaches he showed about eight years ago at the Paula Cooper Gallery. They were, she reminded me, freely rendered shapes of color floating on grounds of various hues. Puzzled as much by their odd color harmonies as by their amorphous forms, she asked LeWitt what the system was he used to make them. "Sol just smiled and said, 'Well, I choose whatever color I like, then I put it next to another one I like.'" Even when systems are more apparently integral to his work, Steir said, "he is never religious about them." He has had no qualms about subverting them if a better idea turns up while he works on a piece. In such instances, as Steir put it, "he would let the work take whatever direction it desired."

When asked to compare working methods, Robert Mangold focused on his friend's use of assistants to execute his wall drawings: "Sol leaves a lot of leeway for the people who execute the work. He's the composer and they play the violins. He and I take very different routes there. I don't have assistants. I would never have anyone draw on my painting." Still, there are some similarities in their approaches, Mangold notes. Both make works that follow self-devised rules. Though Mangold does not make wall drawings, he too uses pencil lines in his work, "not just as something underneath the paint surface, but as a real element of it." In that respect, he says, "Sol's wall drawings opened a door for me. I certainly owe him a debt for that."

One LeWitt quality that some artists enjoyed talking about is his sense of humor. According to Mangold, it is paradoxical and a touch anarchic. "Sol always claims that Sylvia [Plimack Mangold] is the abstract artist and that I'm the realist," he says, with evident amusement. "'What could be more abstract than trying to make a three-dimensional tree into a flat drawing?'" he has LeWitt saying of Sylvia's nature-oriented paintings and pastels. "Then he claims that the shapes I use—triangles and squares and circles—are extremely realistic."

⊡

On the late-night bus ride back to Manhattan from LeWitt's 70th birthday party, the quiet was palpable. In some ways, it was a continuation of the silence that Sol LeWitt demanded of those who sought to praise him. Now and then it was broken with wry observations from a few of the exhausted passengers. For many of those aboard, the wreckage of the party was not entirely surprising. After all, they reasoned in retrospect, Sol was an artist who always wanted the focus to be on his art. His behavior in the face of all those attempted encomiums was, alas, all too predictable. That was the consensus, and many of us nodded reflectively. Eight years later, the invitation from the Madison Museum of Contemporary Art to contribute a piece to this catalogue brought back pungent memories of that surreal evening. My talks with the artists who were there made clear that even if Sol denied them opportunity to express themselves then, their respect and admiration for him and his accomplishments remain undiminished.

CHECKLIST FOR THE EXHIBITION

LEWITT X 2

SOL LEWITT: STRUCTURE AND LINE

All works are by Sol LeWitt and are in The LeWitt Collection.

Drawings

DRAWING SERIES I-1/3241/A AND B 1968
Ink on paper
10 ¼ x 20 ¾ inches

ALL TWO-PART COMBINATIONS OF LINES IN FOUR DIRECTIONS AND FOUR COLORS 1970
Marker and pencil on paper
11 ¾ x 19 ½ inches

DRAWING FOR OPEN CUBE STRUCTURE 1971
Ink and pencil on paper
14 ½ x 12 inches

CIRCLES 1972
Ink and pencil on paper
16 x 16 inches

BLACK CIRCLES, RED GRID, YELLOW ARCS FROM FOUR SIDES, AND BLUE ARCS FROM FOUR CORNERS 1972
Ink on paper
16 x 16 inches

ALL COMBINATIONS OF ARCS FROM CORNERS AND SIDES, STRAIGHT LINES, NOT-STRAIGHT LINES, AND BROKEN LINES 1973
Ink and pencil on paper
17 ¼ x 17 ¼ inches

SCHEMATIC DRAWING FOR "INCOMPLETE OPEN CUBES" 1974
Ink on paper
13 x 13 inches

LINES FROM THE LOWER LEFT CORNER OF THE PAGE TO SPECIFIC POINTS 1975
Ink and pencil on paper
18 ¼ x 18 ¼ inches

LINES FROM THE SIDE OF THE PAGE TO SPECIFIC POINTS 1975
Ink and pencil on paper
18 ¼ x 18 ¼ inches

ISOMETRIC DRAWING, from a set of 40 1981
Ink and pencil on paper
19 x 19 inches

ISOMETRIC DRAWING, from a set of 40 1981
Ink and pencil on paper
19 x 19 inches

SCRIBBLES 2005
Pencil on paper
22 ½ x 30 inches

SCRIBBLES 2005
Pencil on paper
22 ½ x 30 inches

SCRIBBLES 2005
Pencil on paper
22 ½ x 30 inches

SCRIBBLES 2005
Pencil on paper
22 ½ x 30 inches

Gouaches

PYRAMID 1986
Gouache on paper
14 ¼ x 21 ½ inches

PYRAMID 1986
Gouache on paper
14 ¼ x 21 ½ inches

ARCS FROM FOUR CORNERS
IN FOUR COLORS 1986
Gouache on paper
19 ¼ x 29 inches

CONTINUOUS FORMS AND COLOR 1988
Gouache on paper
11 x 29 ½ inches

FORM DERIVED FROM A CUBIC RECTANGLE 1989
Gouache on paper
22 x 30 inches

HORIZONTAL AND VERTICAL BANDS OF COLOR 1990
Gouache on paper
16 ½ x 29 ½ inches

FORM DERIVED FROM A CUBIC RECTANGLE 1991
Gouache on paper
22 ¼ x 29 ¾ inches

BANDS OF BLACK AND GRAY LINES
IN FOUR DIRECTIONS (WITHIN A SQUARE) 1992
Gouache on paper
19 ¾ x 19 ¾ inches

CUBE 1997
Gouache on paper
60 ½ x 60 ½ inches

IRREGULAR FORM 1998
Gouache on paper
22 ½ x 30 inches

IRREGULAR FORM 1998
Gouache on paper
22 ½ x 29 ½ inches

IRREGULAR GRID 1999
Gouache on paper
60 ½ x 61 ½ inches

BRUSHSTROKES 2000
Gouache on paper
22 ½ x 29 ½ inches

BRUSHSTROKES 2000
Gouache on paper
22 ½ x 29 ½ inches

HORIZONTAL LINES 1997–2005
Gouache on paper
22 ½ x 30 inches

HORIZONTAL LINES 1997–2005
Gouache on paper
22 ½ x 30 inches

HORIZONTAL LINES 1997–2005
Gouache on paper
22 ½ x 30 inches

HORIZONTAL LINES 1997–2005
Gouache on paper
22 ¾ x 30 inches

HORIZONTAL LINES 2005
Gouache on paper
60 x 77 ¼ inches

HORIZONTAL LINES 2005
Gouache on paper
60 x 58 ½ inches

3-Dimensional Works

MODULAR WALL PIECE WITH CUBE 1965
Painted wood
21 x 96 x 21 inches

FORM DERIVED FROM A CUBE #16 1989
Painted aluminum
39 ½ x 39 ½ x 39 ½ inches

OPEN GEOMETRIC STRUCTURE 2-2 1-1 1991
Painted wood
20 x 29 ½ x 20 inches

HORIZONTAL PROGRESSION #3 1991
Sprayed enamel on aluminum
18 ¼ x 81 ¼ x 18 ¼ inches

MAQUETTE FOR CONCRETE BLOCK STRUCTURE
"IRREGULAR PROGRESSION, HIGH, #7, VERTICAL BLOCKS"
1997
Painted wood
Maquette: 23 ¼ × 26 ¼ × 5 inches; with base: 25 × 32 ½ × 11 inches
Built size: 240 inches high

SPLOTCH #20 2006
Fiberglass
68 × 68 × 68 inches

LEWITT X 2

SELECTIONS FROM THE LEWITT COLLECTION

All works are in The LeWitt Collection.

René Pierre Allain (Canadian, b. 1951)
Side Loophole 1988
Steel, acrylic paint, canvas, wood
54 ½ × 51 × 6 inches

William Anastasi (American, b. 1933)
Without Title 1997
Graphite on paper
22 × 30 inches

Carl Andre (American, b. 1935)
Sawtooth Range 1993
Plastic laminate
Installation size variable, approximately 1 ¼ × 15 ½ × 1 ½ inches

Carl Andre (American, b. 1935) and
Melissa Kretschmer (American, b. 1962)
Cenotaph for Julian Pretto 1996
Sand-limestone blocks, glass, tar, silicone glue
64 × 20 ⅝ × 22 ⅝ inches

Siah Armajani (American, b. Iran, 1939)
Fibonacci Discovery Bridge (model) 1988
Wood, stain
12 ¾ × 8 ½ × 70 inches

Richard Artschwager (American, b. 1923)
Book 1987
Formica on wood
5 × 20 × 12 inches
Published by Brooke Alexander for the benefit of the
New Museum of Contemporary Art, New York,
in an edition of 40

Alice Aycock (American, b. 1946)
From the Story of the Industrial Revolution 1979
Pencil on vellum
14 × 17 inches

Alice Aycock
From the Story of the Industrial Revolution 1979
Pencil on vellum
14 × 17 inches

Bien-U Bae (Korean, b. 1950)
Mountain Series 1999
Gelatin silver print
20 × 24 inches

Bien-U Bae
Mountain Series 1999
Gelatin silver print
20 × 24 inches

Jo Baer (American, b. 1929)
Untitled 1964
Acrylic on paper
8 pieces, numbered 1–8 on verso:
1) 5 × 5 inches; 2) 5 ⅛ × 5 inches; 3) 5 × 5 inches; 4) 4 ⅝ × 5 inches;
5) 4 ¾ × 5 inches; 6) 5 × 5 inches; 7) 5 × 5 inches; 8) 5 × 5 inches

John Baldessari (American, b. 1931)
The Great Artist, from the suite *Ingres and Other Parables* 1971
Black-and-white photograph with photocopy
12 ¾ × 20 ¾ inches

Robert Barry (American, b. 1936)
Untitled 1992
Black-and-white photograph and colored pencil
19 × 19 inches

Bernd and Hilla Becher (German, b. 1931 and 1934, respectively)
Lime Kilns, Meppel, Holland 1963
Black-and-white photograph
11 ¾ × 15 ¾ inches

Bernd and Hilla Becher
Lime Kilns, Dieversburg, Holland 1963
Black-and-white photograph
15 ¾ × 11 ¾ inches

Bernd and Hilla Becher
Lime Kilns, Brielle, Holland 1963
Black-and-white photograph
15 ¾ × 11 ¾ inches

Bernd and Hilla Becher
Lime Kilns, Harlingen, Holland 1963
Black-and-white photograph
11 ¾ × 15 ¾ inches

Max Becher (American, b. Germany, 1964) and
Andrea Robbins (American, b. 1963)
Dachau, East Wall of Gas Chamber 1984
Chromogenic print
29 ¾ × 34 ½ inches

Gene Beery (American, b. 1937)
Out of Style 1961
Oil on Masonite
38 × 48 inches

Mel Bochner (American, b. 1940)
Plan for Orthogonal Square—Model 3 1967
Painted wood
5 ¼ × 7 × 7 inches; with base: 6 ¼ × 12 × 12 inches

Mel Bochner
D1 (Erased and Turned) 1996
Oil on prepared paper
15 × 20 inches

Alighiero Boetti (Italian, 1940–1994)
Untitled 1988
Embroidery, ballpoint ink, marker, and pencil on canvas
57 × 55 inches

Jonathan Borofsky (American, b. 1942)
I Dreamed Someone Cut up My Duchamp Book (2,175,249) 1976
Paint and charcoal on canvasboard
20 × 16 inches

Dove Bradshaw (American, b. 1949)
Angles 2001
Gesso on linen on wood
18 ½ × 21 inches

Sachiko Cho (American, b. Japan, 1955)
Candles 2003
Digital chromogenic print
16 ¾ × 75 ½ inches

Chuck Close (American, b. 1940)
Self-Portrait 2000
111-color screen print on paper
65 ½ × 54 inches
Published by Pace Editions, Inc., in an edition of 80

Thomas Joshua Cooper (Scottish, b. United States, 1946)
Ritual Gardens, Nesscliffe, Schropshire, England 1979
Gelatin silver print
4 ¾ × 6 ⅝ inches

Thomas Joshua Cooper
Ritual Indication, Lathkildale, Derbyshire, England 1978
Gelatin silver print
4 ¾ × 6 ⅝ inches

Thomas Joshua Cooper
A Quality of Dancing, Duke's Quarry, Derbyshire, England 1979
Gelatin silver print
5 × 6 ⅝ inches

Hanne Darboven (German, b. 1941)
Zeichnung (Drawing) 1968
Ink on paper
39 ½ × 27 ½ inches

Franco Dellerba (Italian, b. 1949)
Islam 1 1999
Wood
32 × 32 ½ × 32 ½ inches

Jan Dibbets (Dutch, b. 1941)
The Shadows at Konrad Fischer Gallery 1969
Black-and-white photographs mounted on board, pencil, ink
19 ½ × 25 ½ inches

Tom Doyle (American, b. 1928)
Arca II 1989
Cherry wood
24 × 37 × 21 inches

Jackie Ferrara (American, b. 1929)
A-126 B Pyramid 1974
Wood (Novaply)
27 × 27 × 27 inches

Ian Hamilton Finlay (Scottish, 1925–2006)
Unnatural Pebbles 1981
Cut and polished stone
Freckled Freshet: ½ × 4 × 2 ⅝ inches
Pebbled Brook: 1 ⅛ × 3 ⅛ × 3 ⅝ inches
Stony Stream: 1 ⅛ × 3 × 2 ⅜ inches

Dan Flavin (American, 1933–1996)
Predominantly White and Predominantly Green 1986
Screen print on paper (set of 2)
Each 29 ½ × 41 ¾ inches
Published by Steendrukkerij, Amsterdam,
in an edition of 40

Hamish Fulton (British, b. 1946)
East, South, West, North 1988
Black-and-white photographs with text
15 × 29 ½ inches

Gilbert and George
(Gilbert Proesch, British, b. Italy, 1943;
George Passmore, British, b. 1942)
Call 1984
Black-and-white photographs with photographic dye
95 × 79 inches

Dan Graham (American, b. 1942)
Carl Andre 1966
Typewriting on paper
11 × 8 ½ inches

Dan Graham
Poetry is a Grinding and an Averaging c. 1966
Typewriting on paper
11 × 8 ½ inches

Dan Graham
Exclusion Principal c. 1966
Typewriting on paper
11 × 8 ½ inches

Dan Graham
Row Houses, Bayonne, New Jersey,
from the series *Homes for America* 1966
Color photograph
11 × 14 inches

Nancy Graves (American, 1940–1995)
The Quipu... 1974–76
Lithograph and ink on paper
22 ½ × 30 inches

Hans Haacke (American, b. Germany, 1936)
Condensation Cube 1963–65
Water in Plexiglas box
10 × 10 × 10 inches

David Hayes (American, b. 1931)
Untitled 1997
Mixed media on paper
30 × 22 ¼ inches

Eva Hesse (American, b. Germany, 1926–1970)
Accession V 1967
Galvanized steel, rubber tubing
10 × 10 × 10 inches

Jenny Holzer (American, b. 1950)
Untitled 9, from *Survival* series 1983–85
Cast aluminum
6 × 10 inches

Arlan Huang (American, b. 1948)
Smooth Stone for Grandfather #69 1994
Glass
3 ½ × 8 × 4 inches

Arlan Huang
Smooth Stone for Grandfather #560 1996
Glass
3 × 7 ½ × 4 ¼ inches

Arlan Huang
Smooth Stone for Grandfather #777 1999
Glass
4 ¾ × 8 ½ × 6 inches

Douglas Huebler (American, 1924–1997)
Site Sculpture Project, Duration Piece #10 1969
Typewriting on paper
3 pieces, each 11 × 8 ½ inches

Will Insley (American, b. 1929)
Building No. 2, Interior Building, Space of Death, Plan Oblique 1970–83
Ink on ragboard
40 × 40 inches

Ralph Iwamoto (American, b. 1927)
Quaroctagons Opus 7 "Nightwatch" 1983
Acrylic on canvas
72 × 72 inches

Donald Judd (American, 1928–1994)
Untitled 1965
Painted steel
5 × 68 × 8 ½ inches

Anish Kapoor (British, b. India, 1954)
Racine 1991
Etching
36 × 30 ¾ inches
Published by Crown Point Press, San Francisco,
in an edition of 20

Alex Katz (American, b. 1927)
Allen Ginsberg 1986
Pencil on paper
22 × 15 inches

Robin Heidi Kennedy (American, b. Mexico City, 1956)
Seated Red Mother 1994
Painted plaster
43 × 15 ½ × 21 inches

On Kawara (Japanese, b. 1933)
May 22, 1967 1967
Acrylic on canvas
10 × 13 inches

Kazuko (Kazuko Miyamoto; American, b. Japan, 1942)
Woman on Step Ladder 1987
Antique kimono with iron-on transfer
48 × 48 inches

Fransje Killaars (Dutch, b. 1959)
Untitled 1993
Acrylic on paper
29 ½ × 42 ¼ inches

Joseph Kosuth (American, b. 1945)
Documentation 1968
Ink and collage in bound blank book
8 × 5 ¾ inches

Barry Le Va (American, b. 1941)
Installation Plan, Sonnabend Gallery 1977
Ink on paper
16 ¾ × 22 ⅝ inches

Jane Logemann (American, b. 1942)
Whole-heartedness—Japanese 2002
Ink on paper
27 ½ × 17 inches

Richard Long (British, b. 1945)
A Line in Canada 1974
Photograph
20 × 30 inches

Robert Mangold (American, b. 1937)
Untitled (Blue and Yellow) 1965
Oil on Masonite
11 ½ × 11 ½ inches

Robert Mangold
Red/Green + Within + (variant) 1983
Acrylic and pencil on wood
24 × 25 ½ inches

Sylvia Plimack Mangold (American, b. 1938)
Untitled (Study for "Portrayal") 1979
Oil on canvas
24 × 24 inches

Sylvia Plimack Mangold
Pin Oak at the Pond 1985–86
Color etching on paper
26 × 29 ¼ inches
Published by Brooke Alexander, New York,
in an edition of 50

Brice Marden (American, b. 1938)
Three untitled prints, from the portfolio *Adriatics* 1973
Etching and aquatint on paper
32 ⅝ × 22 ¼ inches each
Published by Parasol Press, New York, in an edition of 40

Mario Merz (Italian, 1925–2003)
(Without Title) 1983
Metal tubing, sheet metal, and paint
8 inches × 95 inches (diameter)

Ree Morton (American, 1936–1977)
Displaced Tree 1972
Watercolor, crayon, graphite on paper
15 × 22 ¼ inches

Ree Morton
The Sergeant Major's Jealousy 1973
Watercolor and graphite on paper
15 × 22 inches

Juan Muñoz (Spanish, 1953–2001)
Double Lamp 1991
Cast bronze
2 parts, each 57 × 12 × 12 inches

Elizabeth Murray (American, b. 1940)
For Eva 2002
Watercolor on paper, staples
14 ¼ × 6 ¾ inches

Shirin Neshat (Iranian, b. 1957)
Fervor 2000
Gelatin silver print
46 ⅞ × 63 ¾ inches
Published by Barbara Gladstone Gallery, New York,
in an edition of 5

Giulio Paolini (Italian, b. 1940)
Sotto Le Stelle 1988
Painted wood, Plexiglas and fabric, brass nails and hooks
Installation size variable, box 15 ½ × 19 × 1 ⅝ inches

Janet Passehl (American, b. 1959)
Untitled 1995
Muslin and plastic buttons
90 × 27 × 27 inches

Henry Pearson (American, b. 1914)
Cabala II 1973
Acrylic on canvas
66 × 78 inches

Adrian Piper (American, b. 1948)
Some Real Drawings 1968
Typewriting, pencil, and red ink on paper, in three-ring binder
13 × 9 ½ inches

Nina Raginsky (Canadian, b. 1941)
Gary Goode, Boy Scout 1974
Hand-tinted black-and-white photograph
10 × 8 inches

Nina Raginsky
Lynn Chrisman, Vancouver Art Student 1975
Hand-tinted black-and-white photograph
10 × 8 inches

Nina Raginsky
Eleanor 1975
Hand-tinted black-and-white photograph
10 × 8 inches

Nina Raginsky
Jeff Cumpstone and Don Cleugh on Saltspring Island 1977
Hand-tinted black-and-white photograph
7 × 5 inches

Nina Raginsky
Mr. Goodlake, n.d.
Hand-tinted black-and-white photograph
10 ½ × 8 ⅜ inches

Nina Raginsky
The Seal, at English Bay, Vancouver, n.d.
Hand-tinted black-and-white photograph
10 × 8 inches

Steve Reich (American, b. 1936)
Clapping Music for Two Performers 1972, recopied 2001
Ink on paper
13 × 9 ¼ inches

Steve Reich
Piano Phase 1966
Ink on paper
13 × 10 ¾ inches

Dorothea Rockburne (Canadian, b. 1932)
Study for Wooing II 1979
Pencil, colored pencil, vellum, rag paper
25 ¼ × 20 ¼ inches

Robert Ryman (American, b. 1930)
Untitled 1964
Oil on linen
7 ½ × 7 ½ inches

Robert Ryman
Untitled print, from the portfolio *Six Aquatints* 1976
Aquatint on paper
35 × 35 inches
Published by Parasol Press, New York,
in an edition of 50

Fred Sandback (American, 1943–2003)
Untitled 1974
Pastel on paper
17 ¾ × 24 inches

Joel Shapiro (American, b. 1941)
Untitled (Six Types of Metal) c. 1970
Tin, zinc, aluminum, magnesium, copper, steel
6 parts, each 2 ½ × 2 ½ × 2 ½ inches

Joel Shapiro
Untitled 1976
Charcoal on paper
38 × 36 ¼ inches

Charles Simonds (American, b. 1945)
Birth 1971
Color photographs mounted on board
12 × 63 inches

Cary Smith (American, b. 1955)
Blue Fire Painting #13 1995
Oil and wax on canvas
30 × 42 inches

Robert Smithson (American, 1938–1973)
Mirror Vortex 1965
Chrome over iron, stainless steel, and mirror
17 × 9 × 9 inches

Eve Sonneman (American, b. 1946)
Tea Shop, Chinatown, New York 1973
Photograph
4 ⅝ × 13 ¼ inches

Wim Starkenburg (Dutch, b. 1947)
Museum 2004
Digital photograph mounted on metal
29 ½ × 39 ⅜ inches

Pat Steir (American, b. 1940)
Black and Blue Sea with Three Spots of Phosphorescence 1997–98
Oil on canvas
72 × 72 inches

Hiroshi Sugimoto (American, b. Japan, 1948)
State Theatre, Sydney 1994
Gelatin silver print
19 × 24 inches

Hiroshi Sugimoto
Fifth Avenue Theatre, Seattle 1997
Gelatin silver print
19 × 24 inches

Marco Tirelli (Italian, b. 1956)
Untitled 1988–89
Charcoal on paper
38 ¾ × 27 inches

JoAnn Verburg (American, b. 1950)
Giardini Diptych 1997
Color photograph
31 × 44 ½ inches

Franz West (Austrian, b. 1947)
Untitled (Sphairos) 1988
Painted papier-mâché
15 × 14 × 20 inches